PSYCHIC DEVELOPMENT

A HOW-TO GUIDE

MARK HOWARD

TABLE OF CONTENTS

For all of you who follow their path in the light.

Looking to learn, grow and help others

WHO IS THIS BOOK FOR?

Over ten years ago, my spirit guide, Hamish came through and announced that big changes would be happening in our realm. These changes were in effect to stop or slow down the self-destruction that we as humans were putting ourselves through. With wars, famine, greed and more and more people using religion as an excuse to hurt and destroy, the Great White Spirit had (basically) decided to step forward.

To do this, rather than just come through with some big BANG and announce "Hey guys, guess what…" approach (which I know for some would have been ideal), that instead, more and more children would be born with the gift of sight and knowing. Likewise, those whose sight has been suppressed or closed will find themselves become open and start to develop.

By flooding our plane with lightworkers and those who are like-minded and spreading the same message of love and light, these issues and concerns would subsequently be addressed and harmony would eventually be brought back to this world.

This is called the AWAKENING.

As such since that day, more and more students have come forward asking for advice, guidance and help with their psychic abilities.

So why the interest in our world or plane? To understand this you need to understand why the earth is here at all and why we are here with it. If you can understand that as souls we continue to learn and develop in order to help achieve and reach our higher being or higher self – to become one and as the best as we can be.

This requires training and you may, for example, need to understand and develop how to be humble in order to reach your next stage. To this effect, we are then given to live a life where our life path would help us to reach that goal. In short, this life you are leading is in the biggest training ground developed.

Now if you can appreciate that the spirit world is the most amazing place to exist. Where anything is possible. Where you can go and do whatever you like. I have multiple conversations with multiple people all at the same time. This world is so amazing and then you are brought to this life plane – in comparison this world would be hell to live in. Maybe that's where the true meaning of Hell on earth comes from!

As you follow your path, you will find that other opportunities and experiences will come about to help you to move forward. We may, in fact, live a number of lives in order to reach our different stages or complete a path. All these would explain why everyone is born with a gift of knowing and sight in order for us to train and to learn.

The issue comes that with society as it is today, we are born into a world of so many different ideas and contradictions. We teach our children in their early years about the likes of Father Christmas, the Easter bunny and even the Tooth

Fairy, only at some stage to rip this away from them and tell them that no these do not exist and that they now to need to follow the socially accepted guidelines laid down.

In fact, many children have imaginary friends and as parents, we seem to encourage this only at some point to tell our children to stop being silly and grow up. If I told you that this imaginary friend is (more than likely) your child's Spirit Guide, would you be so quick as to stop them developing this relationship?

And how would you feel if you just found out that your imaginary friend from all those years ago was in fact not imaginary at all but in fact someone with whom is there to develop and grow throughout your life, guiding and helping you along the way?

The good news is they never go away and wait patiently until we are ready to start working with them again – and this can happen at any time and at any age.

By encouraging our children now we can help future lightworkers come through and bring about changes to our world.

Some years ago, my youngest son came to me one evening complaining of a man sitting at the end of his bed and playing his flute. He said that it was so loud he had trouble getting to sleep and did not know what to do.

Now as a parent I could have easily told him to stop being silly and to go back to bed and get to sleep (sounds familiar?), but instead advised my son to tell the man in question that he had to stop playing his flute and that he had to leave. In fact, I further advised that if he did not, that I would, in fact, come in and tell him to leave myself!

My son, happy with my reply, went back to his room and told this man to leave. After a period of about 2 minutes, my son popped his head around and said "thanks dad, he has gone now" and promptly went back to bed and fell fast asleep.

So this book is in essence for everyone at some point in their life. If you are having strange dreams, starting to see things out of the corner of your eye, or maybe hearing voices at night, then these are all small indications that you are ready to start to develop your psychic path and reignite your relationship with your Spirit Guides.

Maybe you are feeling lost or just feel something is not right. Again all indications that you are ready to start moving forward, but of course it has to be at a time when you are ready.

Some people often ask if once they complete this will they then be Clairvoyant of a Psychic Medium. These are just labels of terms and many (such as clairvoyant) are used out of context and out of term. Consequently, I prefer to use the term Lightworker.

A medium tends to be someone who is living their last life on this planet and is actually tending to be trained as a future spirit guide for some lucky future Lightworker.

You may have heard the phrases Empaths and Sensitives (again a medium will have all those traits as standard), where an empath can feel and actually sense people emotions and emotional states, and sensitives cannot only feel but pick up on other states such as issues or instantly know when something is wrong. In both cases, it's possible for empaths and sensitives to still have psychic abilities.

Recently I was asked by someone if I was Clairvoyant. Being a mental medium (being one who bears all the Clair-senses) I responded by saying that I was, in fact, a Psychic Medium. This seems to throw her, and I realized to my dismay that she had absolutely no idea of what I was talking about.

The problem is bound that the word "Clairvoyant" is often banded around and used in the wrong context. If more so that many people are unaware of the true word and that this causes miss guidance.

So for those who wish to know the true characteristics of Mental Mediumship, the following is a breakdown of the senses that one would have:

CLAIRVOYANCE

Clairvoyant (clear vision) — To reach into another vibrational frequency and visually perceive "within the mind's eye" something existing in that realm.

CLAIRAUDIENCE

Clairaudience (clear audio /hearing) — To perceive sounds or words and extrasensory noise, from sources broadcast from the spiritual or ethereal realm, in the form of "inner ear" or mental tone which are perceived without the aid of the physical ear and beyond the limitations of ordinary time and space.

CLAIRSENTIENCE

Clairsentience (clear sensation or feeling) – To perceive information by a "feeling" within the whole body, without any outer stimuli related to the feeling or information. (Also see Clair empathy)

CLAIRSCENT

Clairscent (clear smelling) – To smell a fragrance/odor of substance or food which is not in one's surroundings. These odors are perceived without the aid of the physical nose and beyond the limitations of ordinary time and space.

CLAIRTANGENCY

Clairtangency (clear touching) — More commonly known as psychometry. To handle an object or touch an area and perceive through the palms of one's hands information about the article or its owner or history that was not previously known by the clairtangency.

CLAIRGUSTANCE

Clairgustance (clear tasting) — To taste a substance without putting anything in one's mouth. It is claimed that those who possess this ability are able to perceive the essence of a substance from the spiritual or ethereal realms through taste.

CLAIREMPATHY

Clairempathy (clear emotion) – An Empath is a person who can psychically tune in to the emotional experience of a person, place or animal. Clairempathy is a type of telepathy to sense or feel within one's self, the attitude, emotion or ailment of another person or entity. Empaths tune into the vibrations and "feel" the tones of the aura.

CHANNEL/CHANNELING

Channel — A person who allows his/her body and mind to be used as a mechanism for etheric world intelligence to bring psychic information or healing energy to others.

These are the traits of Mental Mediumship, and although so people may have one or two of these, a Mental Medium will work on all of these levels to deliver messages.

Although it is good to understand all of this, I really do not want you to get lost or stuck on the "what am I" question and instead work within this book to develop your skill sets. By the end and after training and developing, you will find your answers if it is what you need to know.

There is, however, one group of people that this book is NOT for and if you fall into this then please put this book away and come back to it another time.

If you are looking to develop your psychic skills to become a famous/ celebrity medium then NO. If you want to be famous then become a film star or become a singer. Trust me it will be easier for you to do that than to go down this route.

Opening your psychic abilities is something that should not be taken lightly and needs to be done with respect as a consequence. This book is not designed to make you something you are not. It is here to help you to grow, develop and to answer some of your questions along the way.

HOW TO USE THIS BOOK

This book is designed for ease and to allow you to move through this without too many issues. Each section will be broken down into three main areas:

Each learning section will take you through the outline and background of that subject. As much as it will be easy or tempting to "skip" a section because you feel you may know it already, then I suggest you do not. As I always say, if you learn something new about something you already know then you are one more step closer to becoming an expert.

So do not skip any sections to this book. Instead, come at each with an open and clear mind, and use what you learn with what you may already know.

There are exercises and worksheets that you will need to use and work within each section. Again use these and work on each one before moving on to the next subject. I have also included links to downloading more copies of these worksheets so you can reuse these at any time.

DEVELOPMENT

In some sections, you will be given links to guided meditations which will be needed to be used throughout your development. These are in MP3 format and I suggest downloading to a mobile device so you can then use them anywhere you wish.

You can also find all the links to the meditations and any other downloads in the resources section at the end of this book.

In each meditation, I suggest finding some "me time" and going finding a quiet place in your home where you can sit and relax whilst you go through these meditations. Each one is as important as the next and I have indicated how often you will need to listen or carry out said meditation.

RESOURCES

Firstly, for help and advice and maintaining your development then please forward any questions to me at medium@markhoward.co.za. I would also suggest you join my development newsgroup so that you are kept up to date with new developments and training.

The second is my website which is www.MarkHoward.co.za – again please contact me if you are stuck or have any issues with the download links given in this book.

MEDITATION

"Meditation is one of the ways in which the spiritual man keeps himself awake."

Thomas Merton

If I say mediation, then the first thing you would think of is someone who sits within the lotus position, hands on their lap, pinching the thumb and forefinger and going into a deep trance.

As much as this may seem like the idea mediation position, there are in fact different ways you can meditate and possibly you are already doing some of these meditation techniques without even knowing it.

The goal of mediation is to clear your mind, to relax and give you inner focus. This is why many people who meditate on a regular basis seem to have a more relaxed and positive outlook on life. What's more, they seem to live longer and look younger than their years.

Mediation should be carried out at a time and location that is suited to you. So even if you are on the beach watching the sea you can still go into a meditative state. There have been times when I have been driving and I have in fact gone into a meditative state and used this time to focus my energies on any issues I'm having or needing to find answers to questions I may have. I also tend to use this time to speak with my guides to create stronger bonds and connections with them.

One well known UK Psychic Medium, Colin Fry, would get his students to sit and meditate with their eyes open. This may seem a little extreme but what he was in fact teaching is for his students to become totally focused in their mediations (it also enabled them to strengthen their third eye).

I even had one person who was advised that the best way to meditate is to lay on a bed with their right arm in the air. They said that they had the most amazing meditations until I pointed out that laying on a bed was, in fact, going to sleep regardless if they had their arm in the air or not!

Sleep too, that point where you are still vaguely aware of what's going on around you but you have those moments where you are drifting, is possibly one of the deepest forms you can go when you first start looking at meditation. Again just remember this is just before you fall asleep so not always recommended.

Meditations are not about going as 'deep' as you can but allowing yourself to focus and clear. This can be done at any level of meditation and allows you to tune with your guides and even loved ones that have passed into spirit.

When meditation starts and ends, I always recommend you to meditate within the red. This means that you only open your root chakra which is red (more about chakras later in this book) and allow yourself to be immersed in the redness around you. This allows you to be fully grounded within meditation too and is a great form of protection.

Within this book, you will be given links to online guided meditations for downloading, in the different chapters. Being guided means you can sit and listen to these as and when you need to and visualize what I'm telling you in your mind. This visualization is the start of working with your third eye and they more you do it the quicker you will become used to using this and opening it too.

Finally, when meditating I always suggest having a white candle lit near you – the small white tea candles that you can purchase are just as good as any for this. This will help with the connectivity with your spirit guides

The following diagram is a little fun and something I designed to easily see the best way to meditate. If you would like to download a colour copy of this please use this link –
http://bit.ly/2tqFmyi

9 Easy Steps

FOR RELAXING & EFFECTIVE MEDITATION

1 Meditate within your own space

Find a quiet place where you can be alone without interruption for around 10 minutes

2 Grab some "me time"

If you have family then make sure it's done at a quiet time or ask them to allow some "me time"

3 Ditch the clock

It does not matter if you meditate for 5mins or longer as long as you mediate. So lose the watch.

4 Get Comfortable

Sit on the floor (on a pillow) or in a chair and kick of your shoes

5 Avoid using your bed

DO NOT lay on your bed as this is not meditation but sleeping!

6 Create the perfect setting

Darken the room if you wish but it's not necessary. Also light a white candle if you have one.

7 Relax, relax, relax

Gently breathe in and out and take your time....it's not a race!

8 Listen

Use my guided meditations which makes it easy to relax and concentrate.

9 Grab a drink

When you have finished grab a glass of water

The following exercise is very easy and one you can do to get started if you have never meditated before. Do NOT have music playing in the background, instead find a place where you will not be disturbed and have a comfortable seated position. I also suggest for the first few times to do this in a darkened room as this allows for the visualization to be stronger.

1. With your eyes closed start off by visualizing the center of a flower. This center is going to be bright yellow in colour. Look at the details of just this center for a moment and take in all the different physical features of it.

2. Next look at the flower itself. I want you to visualize the petals and see these as the most beautiful blue you have ever seen. Again take in all the different physical features of these petals.

3. Next, look at the stem and see how wonderfully green it is and visualize this as well.

4. Finally look at the whole flower and the three different areas, the yellow center, blue petals, and

green stem. Keep that image in your mind for as long as you can.

When doing this you will find your mind initially wondering but after some practice, you will find that it becomes easier to visualize the flower. The flower itself can be any type that you want it to be.

The longer you can keep this image when you are meditating the better as all we are doing is strengthening your third eye at this stage. Do not worry if you cannot keep the flower image there too long or you are struggling to see the flower - just allow yourself to keep trying.

Finally, do not worry about the time it takes to do this. This tends to take about 5 minutes when you first start and after a while, you will find that you have done anything up to 30 minutes with this simple exercise. Again this is purely about training and preparation for you.

YOUR NOTES AND OBSERVATIONS

9

CLEANSING & GROUNDING

"Flying starts from the ground. The more grounded you are, the higher you fly."

J.R.Rim

One of the most important aspects of working on your psychic abilities and connecting means that you need to ensure that you are grounded and that your chakras are cleaned on a regular basis.

Many light works I meet have issues with sleep, anxiety, depression, and sense of being lost or even out of control and much of this is down to the fact that they do not know how to protect or ground themselves when working in the light.

Even when working in meditation it is always best to work in the red chakra, being the root chakra for grounding and I will cover this later in the next chapter.

Grounding does not have to take long to do and more importantly should be done daily if possible. You will see a massive change in your life if the first thing you do each morning is to ground before starting your daily routine.

Simple things such as wearing red items or even walking around barefoot will help you to ground quickly, and more often I tend to spend most of my days barefoot as I work. Even a red wrist band being worn can help a huge deal, and it's these small changes that will enhance your abilities.

Without grounding and protection, you will be open to a lot of issues and problems in your life and trust me when I say the dangers of ignoring this are very high.

Cleansing you chakras does not have to take too long either and I have prepared for you two easy to use guided meditations that will help you achieve both grounding and cleansing. Even if you download these to your mobile phone and listen as you get ready for your day will make a huge impact.

My advice though is to listen to this in a quick meditation. The reason behind this is that you will hear me say "visualize" a lot in the meditations. This is important to do as I'm starting to develop and open your third eye with this technique and it works wonders.

Other ways for protection would include purchasing Hematite stones or crystals which is an excellent way for quick protection and can be worn as a necklace or just kept somewhere upon your person i.e. your purse or your pocket.

A QUICK NOTE ON CLEANSING CRYSTALS:

Many people ask "how do I clean my crystals and how often should I do this?" The following steps are the easiest way to cleanse crystals:

- Take the crystal in your hand (left or right) and hold it under running water
- Ask the archangels and your guides to cleanse the crystal to give it pure form
- Place the crystal in either Sunlight (for one day) or moonlight (for one night)
- Repeat this process every time someone (other than you) touches the crystal(s) as it will then have their energy on them, not yours)

It is also worth a note at this stage to warn against "Energy Vampires" who are people that tend to drain you of energy when you are around them or even people whom you have issues with and do not get on with too well (there will be a reason for this and most likely due to you seeing them as who they really are).

A simple exercise is to either imagine yourself in a Rose quartz crystal, surround yourself into a red bubble or imagine pulling a show curtain around you. Any of these quick techniques will block person(s) in question and allow you to continue on.

Another form of protection for the home or even your car is to imagine a high wall around the home which is higher than the roof and then imagine taking an eraser and rubbing out the home/car within the wall. It sounds crazy for sure, but we do this a lot and even had instances where our neighbor's homes have been broken into but ours has not! We even had people coming to visit us who have walked straight past our door and not even noticed the house and had to call us asking where we lived.

Grounding Meditation Download - http://bit.ly/2TBk8Zy

Chakra Cleaning Meditation Download - http://bit.ly/2SKppOz

YOUR NOTES AND OBSERVATIONS

USING OUR CHAKRAS

"Each of the seven chakras is governed by spiritual laws, principles of consciousness that we can use to cultivate greater harmony, happiness, and wellbeing in our lives and in the world."

Deepak Chopra

Chakras are the concentrated energy centers of the body. Chakra is a Sanskrit term and it means "wheel" or "disk" and is derived from the root word "cakra". Chakras are spinning wheels of energy/light.

Chakras have the loving responsibility of taking in, incorporating and emanating energy to keep us functioning at optimal levels.

The seven main chakras start from the base of your spine and continue to the crown of your head (see image below) and are represented by the following locations and colouring:

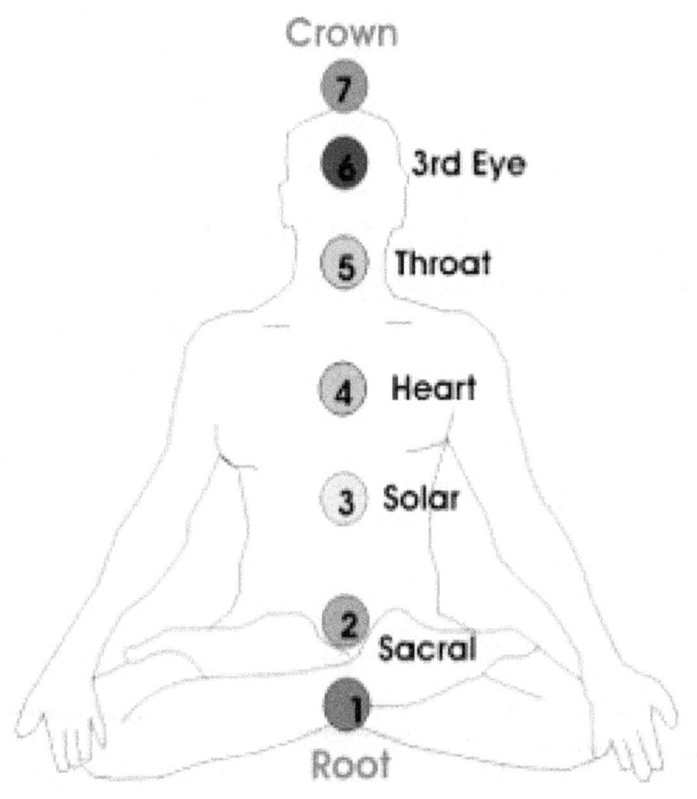

Each chakra is represented by a wheel or disk (as per the image) and represented as follows from the root to the crown:

- (7) Crown – Connection to the Spirit Realm - colour VIOLET/WHITE

- (6) Third Eye – Visual / Clairvoyance - colour PURPLE

- (5) Throat – Communication - colour BLUE
- (4) Heart – Empathy / Love / Emotions - colour GREEN
- (3) Solar – Instincts - colour YELLOW
- (2) Sacral – Creativity - colour ORANGE
- (1) Root – Grounding Chakra – colour RED

When working with your development, your chakras are the most important elements that you can work with – too open on one can lead to issues in your life, likewise being too closed can also lead to problems not developing.

These are the main chakras and to complicate things a little more, each of your ears will also have 7 chakras in them as well as there being seven charkas within each chakra itself – confused? Don't be, you just need to be aware that they are they and that they function well if you manage and look after your main chakras.

Over the years there has been speculation of "other" chakras and these have been speculated upon and some hypothesis being given as well. For now, you do not need to know about these nor work these, with the exception of one chakra.

THE FORGOTTEN CHAKRA

Some years ago, Hamish brought to me a vision of a chakra that I had not seen nor heard about. To be fair at the time I was not even worried about other chakras, new or otherwise and to be shown this was (for me) a revolution in itself.

The Chakra itself was given to me as the "Forgotten Chakra" and sits literally above and almost on top of the Crown chakra.

Unlike the other chakras, this is not a wheel or disk but in essence, an equal lateral triangle of infinite size, and its colour (as I was informed) is a not known on our spectrum but is classed in the spirit world as the purest of all colours.

It is worth being aware of this chakra and you do not need to cleanse it. To its purpose, the only thing I can explain is that once I became aware of its existence and acknowledged it within my cleaning, did I find a change and increase in messages and communication with the spirit realm.

WORKING WITH CHAKRAS

When working with our chakras (and as you will have heard

from the meditation of chakra cleansing), we open our charkas form our root and finish at our crown. The reverse is then done when closing our chakras.

You may ask why do you need to close and the answer is simple. When you do not close you will find that you end up being susceptible to attack from other people and or spirits (negatives), become sick quicker and more often, and even cause issues in your home life with arguments and continued sleep issues.

Many people overlook the importance of our chakras but they are the most important aspect of any psychic and spiritual development work with the most important aspect being our Root chakra. If you do nothing else in your life, this chakra is literally your rock and your support and failure to cleanse, close and work within can cause a lot of issues.

Likewise, once you start working within this chakra, you will find more and more answers being given and open to you at the same time.

OPENING CHAKRAS

As with the mediation, when you open and close your chakras, you visualize lotus petals opening and closing around each. The trouble is, your charkas can easily be open doing day to day activities:

- Through mediations, prayer, and activities such as Yoga
- Exercise (any form no matter how intense or little)
- Walking in Nature
- Walking barefoot (although this is also a good way to ground as well)
- Drinking alcohol (you've heard the biblical phrase "in truth the wine")

Being open is not an issue, the trick is to know when you are too open and when you need to close down. This will come in time as this varies from person to person.

MOTHER NATURE AND OUR CHAKRAS

I was at a talk some years ago where the speaker not only was trying to convince us that the chakras were wrong in the purpose but also we had the colours all wrong as well. Of course, people have these ideas and one doe tend to question when these people come forward with what they consider to be a new ideal.

Troubled by this I asked my guide on how best to see this for others and he advised and explained that the chakras are clearing shown by Mother Nature herself.

In the example, Hamish showed me a rainbow with the colours in it, each section clearly showing the chakras, but for me, the rainbow had the chakras the wrong way around, with red at the top.

As I was then educated and told that a rainbow is not naturally an arc but a sphere and when you take the full spherical shape of a rainbow you will find that the colours match accordingly.

Interesting that the rainbow not only shows us the seven main chakras but also gives us an insight into the eighth chakra or forgotten chakra.

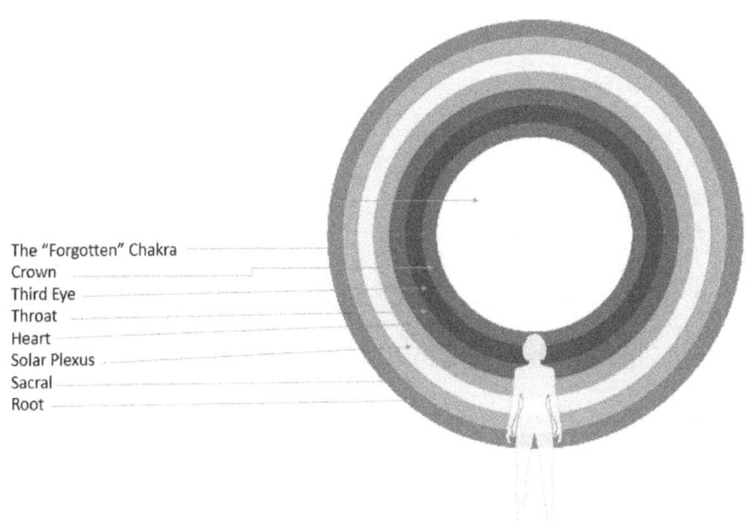

HOW TO USE OUR CHAKRAS

It's possible to use your chakras for everyday use and assistance, and possibly one of the few things that people will do or understand, especially those who will say that the work with the chakras.

FOR EXAMPLE:

Speaking in public or need to put your point across - **Open your Throat Chakra**

Working on a design or crafts - **Open your Sacral Chakra**

You can use combinations so for example, if I'm giving a presentation on a new website I have worked on for my client…

- Open **Throat** for communication
- Open **Sacral** for the design concepts
- Open **Solar** to be in tune with the client
- Open **Third Eye** to visualize clients ideas

By opening up a specific chakra you can help increase your abilities in day to day life as well as help increase your psychic development.

What's more, you can even "boost" your chakras to help with different areas too. One obvious example of that is to watch the news or to watch when someone is speaking such as in politics. The men often wear a blue tie or a blue shirt to emphasis their throat chakras.

When I met one client for a reading I told her that she worked either in design or had something to do with creativity in her work life. She was stunned and turned out she ran a web design company. When she asked how I was able to get that, I pointed out that she wore a lot of orange and a lot of the personal effects she had were also orange.

And it's not just clothing, but jewelry can also help boost. You can try this when you are out with friends and have something with blue on it and see if this helps you within social gatherings or speaking engagements.

Wear different colours to different events and functions and see how these affect your environment and the people around you.

Keep a diary of what happened and how you felt during this time.

YOUR NOTES AND OBSERVATIONS

MEETING YOUR SPIRIT GUIDES

"Your Spirit Guides and Angels will never let you down as you build a rapport with them. In the end, they may be the only ones who don't let you down."

Linda Deir

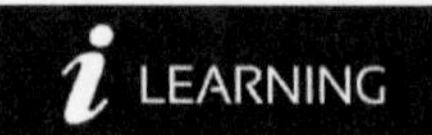 LEARNING

We all have spirit guides since the day we were born. These are our personal life journey mentors who will help and guide us through different paths, challenges, and issues all leaning towards our final goal.

Regardless if you can hear or understand your guide(s) at this time, it is possible that 90% of those reading this book will never hear their guide but understanding them and learning to interact with them is as important to our development and learning to reach our higher true self.

In the introduction to this book, I mentioned about children having imaginary friends and how more often these will be their spirit guides. No matter what guise they come in, they will introduce themselves in a way that is acceptable to you only.

As such they will tend to have the same sense of humor or traits that they will share with us, and may even be a past family member or someone from your past life. What you need to know is that whoever they are, they are with you the moment you take your first ever breath and will continue to be with us throughout our days.

It is also important to understand that you may not necessarily have one guide but a number of guides that will each have a different task, skill or even responsibility throughout your life. Each one is assigned at a time that is needed and when you get to a certain part of your life/path.

WORKING WITH OUR GUIDES

Learning and understanding who and where your guides are from and even have a name seems to be the most common questions asked. With regards to names it's important to understand that in the spirit world, names do not exist more a feeling or knowing about each spirit.

When connecting with your guides in the lesson later, you may ask for your guide's name. They may give it to you if it is a name in a language you understand. Likewise, they may give you a name sounding similar to it or (as in most cases) give you a name that you may call them by.

When working with your guide, you must use the time as if you are speaking to a good friend. Often when I'm driving on my own, I will just naturally speak about my day to my guide, issues or ask questions to build the connection. Being comfortable in doing this is paramount as you will be building trust with your guides (or team).

Your main guide will tend to stand on your right-hand side and that where you will get a lot of indications.

The hardest thing you will need to do is to learn and appreciate Trust with your guides.

TRAINING

Ask yourself who do you trust most in the world, and then ask yourself just how much do you trust them! The truth is you will never trust **anyone** 100% as it is our human nature to be wary of circumstances and other people.

Thinking of this person you trust the most (It may be your partner for example) – just how much do you trust them? 60%....75% it might be even 90%.

In Fact, our trust levels for a person will change constantly depending on the circumstances

Our guides expect nothing less than 100& trust all of the time. They would like us to work together / committed without question and as often as it might seem, they never get frustrated with us.

LEARNING TO LISTEN

- In mediation or a quiet location, ask your main guide to step forward.
- Ask questions that require a Yes or No reply i.e. Are you Male?
- When you ask the question keep your mind free for thought as much as you can.
- Listen for the Yes or No which seems to come from the back of your mind. It may sound distant or even faint. More often it will sound like your own voice at this time – it's not!
- Repeat this Yes and No session on a regular basis.

REMEMBER: Not everyone will have the ability to hear or even see. Over time the voice you hear will go to your right-hand side and sound like someone is talking in your ear. You may then start to pick up accents and other dialects.

If you do not hear then you must go with your gut instincts, feelings and even ask your guides to give you indications such as touching your head or your arm.

All this takes time and may even take years but persistence will work and when it is right you will find the connection with your guide very strong indeed

OUR DOOR KEEPERS

Door Keepers are our protectors our Spiritual bouncers and tend to be located on our left-hand side. More often than not they were powerful warriors or people of great strength when they were present in this plane, and unlike our guides, they tend to be more quiet about who they are and where.

Again you must work with your doorkeeper and gain the trust and support from them. It is also worth noting that they will NOT assist or help you unless you ask. The only exception to this maybe if you get a 'feeling; that going somewhere is not the right course of action and this tends to be more how they will work with people.

Although it is possible to have two doorkeepers it is in fact very rare and something I only found that I had myself back in 2018 when it became apparent that my main guide was also starting to act as a doorkeeper. This was more due to the work and the development I was being taken into meant I was dealing more and more with greater potential dangers and negativity.

Most people and strangely must lightworkers are even aware of the existence of doorkeepers or who their doorkeeper is, but you will find those people who say you have strong energy around you will be picking up on your doorkeeper.

Likewise, children and animals too will pick up on your doorkeeper as their energy and presence are that much stronger.

WANDERING GUIDES

Wandering guides are those that may come to you for a short period of time to assist or to work within a certain segment of your development.

They tend not to stay long term and maybe with you for a few weeks or even months. Once you have completed the work with you they then tend to move on and may come back at a later stage in your development.

Unlike our guides that are assigned to us, these wandering guides tend to work with a number of lightworkers at any given time.

Download the following meditation 'Meeting your Guide(s)' and use this at least once a week. Do not time the session but allow at least 30 mins.

During the session, you will need to 'visualize' everything that I will be saying to you, in your mind. Do not force this but allow yourself to work within the guided meditation.

Have a white candle lit during the session (white tea candles work well).

http://bit.ly/2Ottrtx

YOUR NOTES AND OBSERVATIONS

THIRD EYE DEVELOPMENT

"It is very easy to conform to what your society or your parents and teachers tell you. That is a safe and easy way of existing, but that is not living. To live is to find out for yourself what is true."

Jiddu Krishnamurti

The **third eye** refers to the gate that leads to inner realms and spaces of higher consciousness. The **third eye** often symbolizes a state of enlightenment or the evocation of mental images having deeply personal spiritual or psychological significance.

There seems to be so much mystery surrounding this and (like most things in life) is totally unwarranted. The third eye is located within the middle of our brow or forehead and is known as the 6th Chakra (indicated by the colour purple).

You may have already heard of the phrase 'Clairvoyant' and unfortunately the most miss-used word in the spiritual community. It refers to the third eye and the ability to use this to get visual messages from your guides and to mentally assist in seeing spirit.

Everyone has the ability to use their third eye and is much as a sense as with your other 5 senses, and as with your other senses. You can use your third eye and get information with your eyes open and with your eyes closed.

It tends to be a lot harder with your eyes open when you first start working with your third eye, and as part of the getting you to started, you may have noted that in the meditations I will say the phrase "I want you to imagine" or use the word visualize. This is the start of getting your third eye used to seeing images in your mind.

TRAINING

- Find a quiet place to sit and relax and if possible do this is a semi-dark room if possible.

- Ask your guide to step forward and to start to give you images using your third eye.

- You may start to see static images flash before your eyes or even moving images like you are watching a silent movie. These may be in colour or black and white.

- Do not concern yourself about what you are seeing, but at the end of the session make some notes of what you have seen (no matter how strange it may seem)

- Do not force this – if you do not see anything at the start do not worry. The more relaxed you are the better. It takes time and will happen

HOW TO USE YOUR THIRD EYE

Visualization is the easiest form of communication (after speaking and hearing), and we often express ourselves using our hands such as pointing) in our daily routines.

Once your third eye is 'open' and you feel comfortable working with it you will be able to use it a number of ways such as:

- Getting messages about the future or even current connections with someone
- We can use our third eye to get more information about our guides
- Can be used for confirmation of passed loved ones

Once the connection is strong you will start to see images or scenes 'flash' before your eyes and although they may be quick you will see instantly enough information to pass this on.

One example of this was demonstrated by the late and great Colin Fry, a UK Spiritual Medium whose development and gifts were unprecedented.

In one of his shows (available on YouTube) he brought forward a passed loved one for one of the audience members. As he was giving messages and information he clearly says *"….and this young man is showing me in my third eye how he…."*

A clear and concise example of how Mediums use their third eye along with all of their senses to pass and give information about loved ones.

OPENING OUR THIRD EYE

- You need a Clear Quartz crystal "point" or "wand" before you start

- Take yourself into meditation – to start with clear your mind and keep it blank as much as you can.
- Visualize a flower with bright blue petals, yellow center, and healthy green steam and leaves
- Take your crystal into your hand (either one) move it across your third eye starting from the bottom to the top
- As you do this simply say "Open my third eye" and visualize your eye-opening.
- Repeat this process of moving the crystal and opening your third eye for about 5 - 10 times.
- Carry on your meditation and work with meeting your guides
- Repeat daily for about 10 – 14 days

QUICK NOTE ON CRYSTALS

You will be using your crystal point a lot and you may (over time) by using other crystals with your work. Each crystal needs to be 'cleansed' and 'charged' before you start working with them.

- Take you crystal in your hand and ask your guides to step forward for the cleansing

- Ask that the crystal be used for good intention and then place the crystal under running water (still in your hand)

- Ask the crystal to be cleansed to its purest form.

- Once completed take the crystal and place it for one day in the sunlight or for one night in the moonlight (full moon is best)

- Your crystal is charged and ready to use.

YOUR NOTES AND OBSERVATIONS

DREAM DEVELOPMENT

"All our dreams can come true if we have the courage to pursue them."

Walt Disney

Understand that *everyone* dreams! Often I get told "but I don't dream" and the answer is yes you do....you just do not remember them!

As you are working on your third eye development, you will start to find that dreams will become more often and stronger over the coming weeks, but what exactly arc dreams and why do we want to develop them?

To start with our guides can use "deep meditation" as a time for training, communication and connecting with us. Although sleeping is not meditation, the point just before we enter into REM (rapid eye movement) is the deepest meditation point we can easily achieve, very quickly.

Secondly, loved ones can also come through and communicate with us directly through our dreams. If it is to give messages or send love, dreams again are the easiest way that they can communicate with us.

Finally, it is a way for us to develop our Psychic abilities as upcoming events can be triggered through our dreams and being able to recall these dreams allow us to give clear messages. Now not everyone will be able to do this, but you will to some level of degree years be able to get messages and information through recording your dreams.

One example of this that happened to me involved a dream in which I seemed to be interviewing two school girls. Both were dressed in a very distinctive school uniform and one had this amazing red coloured hair and both looked to be no more than fifteen years of age.

In the dream, I asked a very simple question – "Where is she?" Sounds strange but the two girls looked at each other and the one with the red hair looked at me and said: "if you mean Natalie, you can find her in Paris".

The following month a fifteen-year-old school girl with red hair disappeared with her school teacher. Her parents were beside themselves and even though every port and exit to the UK was on the lookout for these two people, they simply had vanished.

I informed people that the girl in questions will be found safe and well in Paris by the weekend and true to the dream, the girl and the teacher were both identified I a café in Paris.

DREAM STATES

We actually have two different dream states that we dream – one which is called lucid dreaming and the other I have called Vision dreaming. The two are very different in how they work and both can easily be determined from the other.

Lucid Dreaming – This is what I call our daily mind dump. All the information we have stored in the last few days in our memories and all those pieces that really are not important tends to come out in these dreams.

Often you will feel uncomfortable in the dreams, maybe doing strange things such as flying or running (towards or away), nothing in it will make any sense and more often than not you will not remember any of these dreams.

One of the issues with lucid dreams is that loved ones can come through in these and vision dreams which can complicate things and makes it doubly important to make notes on your dreams.

I these cases the one thing I always advise is to look at what the person is wearing and take note of any specific colours around then. Match these colours to your chakras so if you see a lot of blue then maybe there is an issue or the need to communicate with someone and so on.

Vision dreams – these are different in that they tend to be created with our guides for training purposes. Often they feel so real, that when you wake up you are not sure if you were dreaming or not, or may even be surprised to find yourself in bed.

You tend to recall these dreams days later with clarity although there is one exception to this rule. In some training cases, you may need to go through this and the training recollection is removed from you i.e. you won't recall the dream. Then at the time that is right, this will come through in your daily life.

In this case, you may not recall the dream of training as mentioned but when you awake you will feel as if you have had no sleep despite having your usual amount of sleep time.

Taking all this into account, you will find that the more your abilities grow and the more you connect with your guides through your dreams, the more you will find that waking up at 3 am in the morning for no apparent reason starts to become a normal part of your sleep patterns.

As you start to develop these dreams you may become aware of your guides appearing in them and that you may start to establish a closer and stronger connection with them at the same time.

DREAM TYPES

WATER, WATER, EVERYWHERE!

Water plays a big part in our dreams – sometimes for the good and sometimes we feel negative (nightmares). There is a reason why you will start to have more and more dreams of water!

As our spiritual mind starts to grow and develop, our logical mind tends to fight back and causes us to self-doubt about what's going on. One way this occurs is by using nightmares as a way to control what we are doing.

Water plays a big part in dreams and often signifies the following:

- Water is used for spiritual birth or rebirth
- It will appear in different ways from rivers to swimming pools, even water from taps
- Water turning from sludge to clear water or even drowning are all aspects of spiritual development.
- The feeling of drowning can also be a sign of rebirth

PLANES, TRAINS, AND AUTOMOBILES

Travel also plays a big part in our dreams and is often used as a way to work with something we all know about i.e. being in a car. Do not confuse dreams of being late for a plane though with the following.

- Our guides may meet us by traveling in cars for example

- You may have dreams of being out of control in a car

- Trains also play a part in passing on messages in a dream. You may meet someone you know who has a request or needs a message passed on

- Feeling of not getting on a plane or similar is more likely to do with what is going on in your life at that time

- Remember to use your chakra colours – a blue car may indicate an issue with communication or a change in your communication as well!

YOUR SPIRITUAL HOME

Each of us has a spiritual home and this tends to be a safe haven in or dreams where we can meet our guides and others that we allow into the home.

You may possibly already bee to this home or dreamt of being in a house or location that you simply felt safe within. You may also felt that some rooms of the house you did not want to go into and felt uneasy about – these tend to be new training and new concepts in your life coming up and as such your logical mind will feed on the fear of the unknown to stop you going into these rooms.

- It may start off small but will build even to the size of a city

- You will have a sense of belonging although you will not recognize the house or building

- There will be rooms you are too scared to go into

- You will only go to your spiritual home in a visionary dream

- You tend to be with your guides and often with your doorkeepers when you do.

- There is normally a message rather than training when you go to your home.

- Sometimes, loved ones may meet you here as well

TRAINING

When you awake, you will recall some of your dream (lucid) or most of it (visionary). The mistake people make is that they go back to sleep and they will forget their dream(s)!

- Keep a notepad and pen/pencil by the side of your bed – this is your dream journal

- When you awake make notes, bullet points and just a few lines which will be enough for you to recall the dream

- When you get up in the morning make more detailed notes for your nights' scribblings as soon as you can

- Do not worry if you do not recall everything in the dream – as much as you can is the most important thing

Place the clear quartz crystal under your pillow at night (the one you use to open your third eye) as this will help to enhance your dream state.

One of my students (who also said she did no dream) said that she got some amazing results from doing this. I asked her if her husband dreams and she said he did not. I asked her to put the crystal under his pillow without him knowing to see what would happen. The following day she called me to say her husband woke up ad said that he had the most amazing dreams!

YOUR NOTES AND OBSERVATIONS

57

CONNECTION

"We cannot live only for ourselves. A thousand fibers connect us with our fellow men; and among those fibers, as sympathetic threads, our actions run as causes, and they come back to us as effects."

Herman Melville

Connecting with people may seem a strange thing to do, but in essence, it is required for creating a bond in order for you to understand people better as well as being able to assist with your development, especially in the early days of working.

As you develop you will find that you will connect with people automatically or find that a connection is there from an existing bond or even relationship. You will need to understand when you are connected and more importantly how to disconnect from a person.

In social environments, connections can happen very easily due to alcohol intake or taking other substances. It's the reason why people may suddenly have strange desires to do things that they otherwise would not do or have feelings for someone that they never had before.

This demonstrates how careful you need to be and the following is the process I teach students for connecting when carrying out readings for their clients.

CONNECTION PROCESS

1. Imagine a cord similar to an umbilical cord coming out of your navel.

2. Wrap the cord around your body from left to right. So it will go under your left arm around your back and out under your right arm.

3. Now visualize the cord connecting to the person in question in the photo or to the person you want to connect with.

4. Have the cord go under their right arm, around their back and back under their left arm, before connecting to the person's navel.

5. In essence, you have started to create an infinity symbol between you but it's not completed (see the image on this page)

Once you are connected with someone you will find that images start to come to your third eye very quickly or you have feelings about situations, anxiety, fears or even passions. All these will be of the person you have connected to and will not be your feelings.

The connection also does not require you to be in the same room as the person, as this technique can also be used for distance as well. All you really need for distance is the person's name and then follow the steps for connection.

Again with distance connections, you need to be careful and you must also be careful with whom you connect with. Other psychics and lightworkers will know if you connect ad they may block or use your connection to find out who you are.

This happened to me when I first started to put together my website for my mediumship. Looking for inspiration I took a look at one of the celebrity mediums on the UK's website to get ideas and to see how she went about doing certain sections.

In essence, as I was thinking of this lady, I had in fact created a connection with her and at the time had not realized what I had done. To spare my blushes, I won't go into many details but let's say the medium in question later came through clear as day to my third eye not looking very happy with me due to the unwarranted connection.

Once you understand how easy it is to connect, then you need to learn and recognize when you are connected and how to break the connection from the person in question

BREAKING THE CONNECTION.

Once you have completed the work, it is fundamentally important that you break this connection before doing anything else. If you remain connected to the person you will find yourself unable to sleep or find yourself continuing to think about the person in question.

To break simply imagine taking some scissors and cutting the cord. Once you have done this ask Archangel Michael to heal and bless the severed connections.

IMPORTANT NOTES ABOUT CONNECTIONS

- If you connect with passed loved ones or spirit be careful about who you connect too as you might pick up on their past issues. Suicides, for example, are very dangerous and you may have these tendencies if you do not disconnect ASAP. If in doubt call your doorkeeper forward, break the connection and then ask Archangel Michael to heal and bless the severed connections.

- If someone blocks you then break the connection and leave it. There is a good reason they have blocked you so walk away.

- DO NOT use this method to connect with your spirit guide(s) and/or doorkeeper. They will not allow it and will automatically block you with trying that type of connection.

YOUR NOTES AND OBSERVATIONS

65

WORKING WITH AND READING AURAS

"The aura given out by a person or object is as much a part of them as their flesh."

Lucian Freud

Every living thing has an aura – be it your friends, pets, animals and even plant life will all give off a natural energy field around them. Science has in the past few years (finally) admitted that the aura exists and that there are different layers and colours associated with each one.

It's good to know that science finally caught up with something that has been used and worked with by people for other a thousand years

When working with the Aura you will start to see colours around a person. These will sometime be just the one colour, merge or a mixture of colours, depending on the person and what they are going through at that time.

The colours surrounding your body might change several times a day. The energy reflects how you feel and will change with your mood. For people, several different colours appear within their energy field at one time.

This is why it is always hard when someone asks you to read their aura as it really depends on what they are going through will depend on the colours around them.

Colours and intensity of the aura, especially around and above the head can have VERY special meanings. Watching someone's aura you can actually see the other person's thoughts before you hear them expressed verbally. If they do not agree with what this person is saying, you effectively see a lie every time. No one can lie in front of you undetected. We cannot fake the Aura. It shows our True Nature and intentions for everyone to see.

This may already be happening to you when you for unknown reasons seem to know when someone is not telling the truth.

There are seven layers of the aura and the easiest one to see is layer one and these are the white base layer around a person. Note that white seen elsewhere above the base can be a different indication or if you see their base being a very intense whiteness. In this case please refer to the colours table in this section for the different meanings.

READING A PERSON'S AURA

When you have found the person whose aura you want to read, stand facing them, close your eyes and take several deep breaths. When you feel ready to open your eyes again, stare at the person, making sure you feel as though you are almost seeing straight through them (another technique is to look slightly to the left or right of the person's forehead). You will then see the figure in front of you start to blur.

One of the first colours you will see will be the white first layer. Soon after other colours may start to appear in splodges. If you can't see them, imagine a colour instead. The first colour to pop into your mind is more often than not the colour of the subject's aura. Rub your hands together, and then place them above the person's head.

Slowly move your hands towards and away from the head, and once you have linked with the aura you may feel a sensation of tingling, heat or even coldness. With practice, you will learn how to relate the sensations and colours you pick up to specific things going on in someone's life.

TOUCHING THE AURA

As well as seeing the aura it is possible to touch and work the person's aura in readings and healing.

With the person laying down or sitting in the chair, feel just outside their Aura field and gently push your hand forward. You should feel a slight "bubble" effect around the person and this may change in height and depth depending on what's going on with the person.

- A dip in the aura may indicate an unbalanced chakra
- Heat or sudden cold may indicate a past trauma to the area or potential trauma that needs to be looked at for the future
- Connect with your guides and ask them to guide your movements and give you any information on what you are feeling or sensing.

For myself, I tend to feel the heat around areas and in one reading felt intense heat around the person's pelvis, knees and ankles which indicated some kind of trauma. I questioned this with my guide and was advised that the person in question had fallen down a deep hole and landed on the feet causing the issues that they were now having in their legs.

When I asked about this it turns out the person had fallen down a ten-foot hole and had massive trauma to the areas that I had found as indicated by their aura.

The following is a technique used to practice reading your own aura. This can be more helpful and valuable to you because you are not watching someone else who could become restless and impatient. But at the same time, many people have difficulty in being objective with themselves. This exercise should be used to practice seeing the aura and not necessarily interpreting it.

Sit in front of a mirror. Begin by looking at your shoulder and neck area in the mirror. Let your eyes go out of focus as if you were looking beyond your body's reflection. After some practice, you should begin to see a white glow or outline, about 1 to 2 inches wide, around the shoulder and neck. This is your inner-aura.

The following table is some of the colours and meanings that I have found reading aura for clients. Please use these meanings as a base for yourself and other time you will develop your own meanings or even add to those within the table

Red	Green	Pink
Passionate, courageous, strong Use red to for "get and up and go"	Affectionate, loyal, trustworthy Use green to promote calm, relaxation, healing and balance	Charming, peacemaker, full of love and compassion Use pink to attract love, protection, and security
Orange	**White**	**Blue**
Joyful, happy, optimistic, independent, social Use orange to give you confidence	Spiritual person, idealist, innovator, sometimes shy, seeking or aware of enlightenment	Communication, listener, self-expression Use blue to attract tranquillity and to learn to communicate

Yellow	Black	Purple
Creative, artistic, is to open, over-analyzing Use yellow to bring happiness in your life and strengthen intuition	Seeking knowledge, intense, introspective, hidden depths. Use black to look within	Strong, sensitive, spiritual and intuitive. Use purple to develop your spiritual side
Grey	**Gold**	**Brown**
Can reveal that someone feels trapped.	Highly spiritual, working with the divine.	Down-to-earth, grounded personality.

YOUR NOTES AND OBSERVATIONS

75

READING PHOTOS

"A tear contains an ocean. A photographer is aware of the tiny moments in a person's life that reveal greater truths."

Anon

Using a person's photo is a great way to develop your connectivity as well as strengthen your connection with your guide and consequently develop your psychic abilities.

Much of my work is around photo readings and I have been asked to do this for online dating profiles, partners, loved ones who passed away and even with helping with Police investigations.

More recently I have been asked to do these readings so that clients can better understand how other people see them and how they should interact better with their peers in certain situations. In short, photos readings have a lot to offer for many people.

CONNECT WITH A LOVED ONE IN SPIRIT

Connecting with a loved one in spirit can be done in a number of ways, but a photo is one of the easiest. A psychic can bring a person through and give evidential information along with confirmation of events and timeframes.

Although it's rare for a person to ask for a connection this way (after all most Psychic Mediums can connect directly spirits), I have had this during a reading where the person wanted me to connect with someone specific who was a friend rather than a family member, and produced a photo for me to look at.

WORKING WITH PHOTOS

Working with photos may seem hard to do but all you need is the person's name (no date of birth is needed), why the reading is required and then connect to the person in the photo as you would as outlined in the chapter on the connection. It is also worth noting that the majority of your photo readings if not all of them will, in fact, require distance connectivity.

The thing you will find is that you will tend to focus your energies on the eyes of the person as the eyes cannot lie. You may also start to see aura colours appearing, but for much of this work, you will be asking questions on your guides and making notes on what you are being told.

- Take absolutely no notice of what is going on in the photo
- Go with your gut instincts if at this stage you cannot hear
- Your first impression will normally be the correct one.
- Use your third eye and make note of any images – they will be correct
- Use your natural instincts. Your feelings, smell and taste can all add to the reading.
- Ask questions of your guide
- Remember to disconnect once you have completed the reading.

Again you can ask questions that form a base to your reading and the following are good questions to start with.

- Is the person happy in their life
- Are there any issues past or present that are hindering them
- How are they socially with friend/family
- How do they treat people or interact with them
- If in spirit how old were they when they passed
- How did they pass

- And so on….

As you develop you may find that much of your written readings will see you being 'Shadowed'. This is where your guide will, in fact, take over the reading and although you are aware of the typing and what's going on see a little spaced out or feel you are not 100% connected to yourself.

You will do more of this type of writing in the chapter on automatic writing in this book.

EXAMPLE READING

I once saw an article in the UK national press about a young lady who asked a "psychic" to do a photo reading of her. The photo she provided was at best a distant holiday snap which in fairness should have been the reader's first issue (a closeup headshot is always best as you need to see the eyes).

The reading itself was more a list of things that the girl in the picture likes such as "she liked chocolate ice-cream" and that she has had teeth whitened. This is not a reading, and as much as I would like to say that was a one-off, I have seen more and more photo readings and even psychic readings being done in the same manner.

The following is a small part of a photo reading I gave of a young lady some years ago. For obvious reasons I have not added the photo to this reading, but you will see how the reading is laid out and the information provided at that time. I have also not included the full reading as it does go into more personal details as well:

This lady shows independence and determination around her. Someone who is desperate to succeed against all the odds and someone who will battle and show that she can fight against anything that is thrown at her.

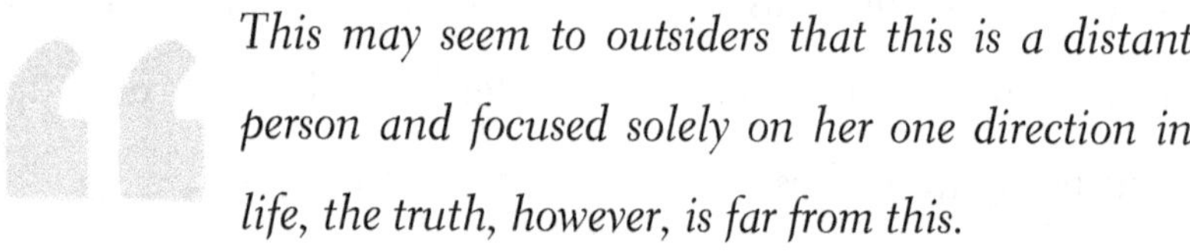

This may seem to outsiders that this is a distant person and focused solely on her one direction in life, the truth, however, is far from this.

Her determination and drive have come from a past situation or circumstances that she currently uses to protect herself and those she is close too.

She may distance herself quickly if she feels threatened or in a situation, she cannot control. She may even use distraction or redirection to avoid people from getting close or to direct people away from her.

The shame is deep down she is a different person. Someone who is crying out to be loved and more importantly understood.

She will continue to block and build walls until she knows and understands what it is she is looking for in life and this will be hard because in herself she really does not know or understand. She needs to be more open and honest with herself and others around her before this will happen.

Yes, she will be successful in what she does in her life, but deep down she will always feel alone. There is also fear around her – it is someone she is close to and possibly the only person she can relate too. This person is older and possibly a family member. The fear is a loss – loss of someone she really needs by her day and night.......

This level of reading is the least I would expect from my students and from anyone offering to do readings. Again asking questions over and over will help you get to this level.

The only real way to train and develop your photo reading skills to do this. To start with, work with friends' photos and ask them if it's ok if you can do them a reading. Be honest and tell them that you are starting out and looking to develop this skill.

Keep the reading light and just give what's given to you. You will find these readings slightly hard to do as you will know about the person in question already but will help you develop and grow with confidence as you do these for other people.

Key the thing is to remember the following:

- **Listen** – remember not everyone can hear but it is still a good idea to carry on listening whenever you are doing any kind of psychic work.
- **Look** – using your third eye record any images that come through
- **Instinct** – again a good way for our guides to give us accurate information is purely through our instincts and how we feel

As always the biggest fear we have is self-doubt and over-thinking the reading. Remember, when your connection becomes stronger it is even possible for you to be in a "shadowing" with your guide so that they can write information down.

YOUR NOTES AND OBSERVATIONS

86

PAST LIFE REGRESSION

"The past is never where you think you left it."

Katherine Anne Porter

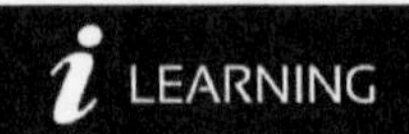

Past life regression and working with past lives helps you to understand where you have come from and where you are going. There is also the chance that your guide(s) where present from your past life and may have even been a family member or an active part of it.

Have you ever wondered why certain things seem to keep happening in your life for no apparent reason? What about those strange dreams that seem so real, you are convinced you were there? Or maybe you have some unexplained birthmarks or even "phantom pains" that just won't go away.

All these could be signs on a past life that is trying to get through to you, repressed memories trying to resurface leaving you more confused than actually giving you answers.

By doing this you get to understand more about yourself and your guide(s) at the same time, building that all-important connection that will bring you closer and develop your abilities.

Everyone has a past life and in fact, we can have up to seven past lives and each one may contain information about why you do certain things or why certain situations keep on happening to you. It is also rare that karma from a past life will be still affecting you today as this would have been taken away when you initially passed back over.

At the start of this book, I explained how this world is our training ground in preparation to reach our higher selves. This learning cannot be completed in one session and depending on what you are seeking to achieve may take place over more than one lifetime. This is part of the reason that many people believe they are carrying past life karma when in fact they are actually completing their learning.

It would also explain why some people pass so quickly or so young, where learning may require a life span plus part of another to complete it. In these circumstances, it is not normal for a person to go back to the spirit world but instead to be re-born or re-incarnated back to continue their learning processes.

KARMIC DEBT

So let's get this one cleared up first – you do NOT bring with you past Karmatic debt into your life. What you will most likely bring is continued experiences or training that will help you to reach your higher self.

Often I hear people say that they are suffering due to a past life debt – rubbish. They are possibly suffering because they are failing to learn from their past life experience or indeed not helping themselves to develop and gain knowledge

SOUL MATES. TWIN FLAMES AND SOUL CIRCLES

You may have heard of this phrase, maybe even someone has said this to you. You feel a strong connection and everything just feels right and you know immediately you have met your twin flame.

The problem is what you think is a twin flame and what one is might actually come as a shock to you. I for one was not aware of the implications until in a recent reading, my guides took over the reading and gave very specific points on what twin flames are.

The reading started off as follows

"…Twin flames are a phrase that is often used out of context and one that you need to be careful of. Twin flames are not about romance (although this can be confused with such as to the intensity).

Twin flames are those people who have a connection and can be with the same sex or the opposite sex. These are mirror images of ourselves and often than not are a connection to a past life or past event.

A twin is normally a past family member and can be a brother or sister that you had in a past life, but due to the connection and the family love that is given, this more often gets confused. This is why many twins who embark on a romantic nature may get hurt or get divided as the universe will naturally pull you apart. This is hard but we do this for your own good.

Twins can come into your life as a lesson, or as part of each other's journey to help each other get to where you need to go."

So from the start, it's apparent that twin flames are not a romantic connection and past or present, which many people are lead to believe and (as you can read) can get confusing with the love that is felt.

The reading continued with an interesting insight though…

> "….As twins, you have connected always and you will cross each other in your minds, dreams and on your astral journeys. This will not change as with other twins this is the way it is and will remain. You will feel pain, joy and even sorrow at times around your twin. Likewise, they will feel the same around you too. "

This for me now makes sense as to why so many people feel this strong connection and pull. And although not everyone will agree with this insight, it has been a very enlightening eye-opener!

Soul Mates on the overhand is totally different. This will be someone that you have met in your past life or indeed are still to meet. This person will be your soul partner and as you go through your lives, then this person will come back time and time again.

This person will have an immediate attraction and a deep sense of love and belonging. The easiest way I can relay this is from the movie 47 Ronin where Keanu Reeves says to his soul mate:

"I will search for you through a thousand worlds and 10,000 lifetimes until I find you again"

Soul Circles are another source or people or groups that form throughout our path and lives. These "groups" tend to have the same person or persons present and that you will meet again and again.

You might look at someone and feel you have met before. Or you have an instant trust (or even dislike) to someone because they were in your soul circle.

This group is there to support, learn and develop from.

MEDIUMSHIP LIFE SPAN

One of the questions often asked is "what is a medium and am I one?" To answer this then you need to understand that our past lives are developed to reach our higher self.

With this in mind, Mediums tend to be those who have had many lives and are being prepared to become Spirit Guides for lucky future Medium generations. It is an honor and a privilege to get to this level and once you understand means that after this life there will be no more.

THE POLLOCK TWINS – A TRUE PAST LIFE ACCOUNT

The Pollock twins were English girls who are often referenced as proof of reincarnation. Their parents, John and Florence Pollock, lived in Hexham, England. They had two daughters, Joanna, 11, and Jacqueline, 6. On May 5, 1957, the two children were killed in a car accident.

Florence got pregnant the following year and gave birth to twin girls on October 4, 1958. Gillian and Jennifer were identical twins, but they had different birthmarks. Jennifer had a birthmark on her waist that matched a birthmark that Jacqueline had. She also had a birthmark on her forehead that resembled a scar that Jacqueline had.

The family moved to Whitley Bay when the twins were three months old. Two years later, the girls started asking for toys that had belonged to their elder sisters, despite never having seen the toys before.

After the family returned to Hexham, the twins, despite never having been there, pointed out landmarks their older sisters had known.

They also began to panic upon seeing moving cars, shrieking, "The car is coming to get us!" After they turned five, their memories of their previous lives faded, and they went on to lead normal lives.

By connecting to your past life, you are seeking to connect with your most recent or even your most relevant past life (depending on what you are seeking). Past life meditation which is deep and takes up to 90mins to do per session, and it is best to ask questions to help with each session

From this, my guides have developed an easy, self-use past life session system that anyone can use and can be used as many times as you like.

When I first introduced this to my students I was blown by the response and the information that each of the students gave and how they suddenly understood.

To use the guide simply look at each section starting at the top and look at the focal point (the grey circle) for that section and allow your guides to draw your attention to the appropriate location i.e. Yes or No when asking questions

So an example is in the century you are drawn to 1700, years 9 and 40 – this would give you the year 1749 and would be an indication of a year that was important i.e. your initial birth or even passing.

The following mediation can also be used with doing past life regression

http://bit.ly/2Y1yyEc

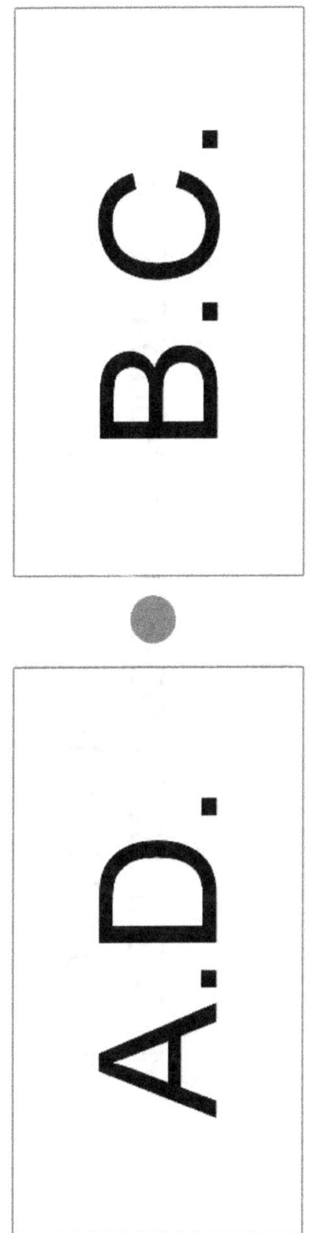
B.C.
A.D.

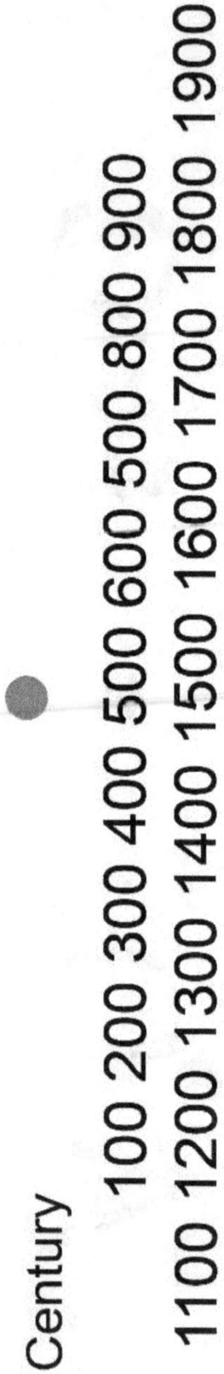

Century

100 200 300 400 500 600 700 800 900

1100 1200 1300 1400 1500 1600 1700 1800 1900

Year   0 1 2 3 4 5 6 7 8 9
10 20 30 40 50 60 70 80 90

NO

YOUR FIRST PAST LIFE READING NOTES

101

When you get to the Yes/No section this is where you ask questions and ask as many that come to mind no matter how silly they may sound.

- Are you male or female?
- What are your initials?
- What is your name?
- What year is it?
- Are you married?
- Do you have a family?
- How many children do you have?
- Do you work?
- What job do you do?
- What are you wearing?
- What nationality are you?
- Where do you live?
- And so on…

After each session, you will find that for the next 24 to 48 hours you will have desires or cravings to do things that you will not normally do. You will also find that you have dreams about the period you went too and even have the odd "recurring" memory pop into your head. All these must be noted as these will have bearings on your past life experience.

In each instance, you must take notes and add these to the notes you made during the past life session

Dreams / Nightmares – Do you have recurring or even vivid dreams? You know where the dream seems so real you actually think you are there.

Birthmarks – Sometimes birthmarks might indicate past live incidents. In one fascinating case, an Indian boy claimed to remember the life of a man named Maha Ram, who was killed with a shotgun fired at close range. This boy had an array of birthmarks in the center of his chest that looked like they could possibly correspond to a shotgun blast.

So the story was checked out. Indeed, there was a man named Maha Ram who was killed by a shotgun blast to the chest. An autopsy report recorded the man's chest wounds — which corresponded directly with the boy's birthmarks

DÉJÀ VU – Most of us have experienced the eerie feeling of – the sudden, surprising feeling that an event we are going through at the moment has happened exactly this way before

With the internet being so at hand today, you can then do further research on your experiences and see how they correspond to the session.

Phantom Pains – Sometime you may get pains that have no sense to them. Maybe you have an acute pain that you cannot explain but have always been with you. This sometime could reveal how you passed in your previous life.

Stabbing pain in your back in the same location could mean you were stabbed. Of course, you should get medical advice but if they cannot find anything then chances are it's a past life issue.

Fears – These too can play a big part in a past life. Fear of water may indicate drowning, fear of heights a fall and even a fear of small spaces could mean you were buried alive...

With one client, he was able to give details about a plane crash, the name of the pilot and even the location, date and time this all happened. Further internet searching confirmed everything in the reading that this client had to be on the plane when it crashed.

105

YOUR NOTES AND OBSERVATIONS

AUTOMATIC WRITING

"You can make anything by writing."

C.S.Lewis

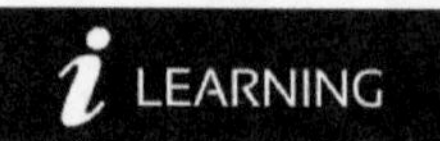

Automatic writing is a way to channel information (including predictions and prophecy) and spiritual energy through writing. It is the ability to allow intuition from outside you to flow through you. Automatic writing is a form of intuition that has been around for thousands of years. But it wasn't until the late 1800s and early 1900's that it became better known through the worldwide spread of the Spiritualism movement.

Automatic writing works, regardless of whether you write on paper or type from a word processor onto a computer screen. Some psychics that have been doing automatic writing for years are more comfortable writing with a pen to paper. There are other psychics that feel that the digital link of a computer allows for a stronger connection.

Automatic writing is sometimes known as "shadowing" when a spirit or your guide will step forward and control your hand and the way the pen moves across the paper or keyboard.

More often I tend to use this for doing email readings and photo readings – this allows for a more accurate representation of the reading for the client.

Automatic writing can be used for:

- Email readings
- Growing your connection with your guide(s)
- Photo Readings
- General writing i.e. blogs
- Giving messages
- Even Writing books

One great example of this is a series of books by Anne Dooley, "The Teachings of Silver Birch" available on Amazon.

These books and more importantly the guidance within them were given to Anne via her guide Silver Birch. She wrote these books in a semi-trance state using automatic writing.

Using automatic writing you can work closely with your guides to find out more about them. Not just their name but their likes, dislikes, how they lived and so on. Of course, they may not wish to give you everything about them, but just by doing the exercise will help you to develop this all-important bond and connection with your guide(s).

1. Determine what method you are most comfortable using. Your preferred method maybe a pen and paper, a computer or any writing implement.

2. Find a calm and quiet place for the meditation - open your chakras and connect with your guides

3. Start to write by drawing a small circle on the page and allowing your hand to run free. You can either ask questions or just allow your guide to writing.

    Don't ask "yes" or "no" specific questions. You are looking for inspiration, advice, and guidance. You can't get Spirit to make decisions for you. You can, in the exercise of your free will, receive information that helps you make the best decisions for yourself.

4. Once you have your questions written, concentrate on them one at a time. You are seeking answers from

higher-energy beings or spirits that have a clearer view than we do in the physical world.

5. If you don't feel that you are making headway, take a break and go back to it!

6. Some people keep their eyes open. Others prefer to keep their eyes closed... Go with your first thoughts. Write anything that pops into your head. Don't stop to think or analyze. Try to keep a continuous flow.

7. Practice makes perfect. Keep trying this daily for 30 days. Attempt to maintain a regular schedule. Do your automatic writing at the same time every day.

8. If you see images pop into your head, then draw these as well as they may have some significance to the session.

DEVELOPMENT

Meditation link: http://bit.ly/35mm6Tz

YOUR NOTES AND OBSERVATIONS

PSYCHIC DRAWING

"I sometimes think there is nothing so delightful as drawing."

Vincent van Gogh

There are many different ways that psychic art can be expressed. Sometimes the drawing or painting can be a likeness to a loved one now in the spirit world. Spirit Guides can also be shown through this type of media. Messages too can be portrayed through psychic art, with drawings that tell a story. The art form can seem to take shape as the pen, pencil or brush moves across the paper.

You will feel compelled to work in a particular way and you may feel that you are inspired to create 'something'. This will be spirit inspirers working with you.

You may feel totally distanced from the outside world during this creative time, and at one with yourself, in complete harmony and peace.

As with automatic writing, psychic artworks on the same principle. Allow your hand to be guided. Don't think about what you are doing, feel what you are doing. Go with the flow, and you will be surprised by the outcome. Never think that you are not good enough to do this type of creative work.

It's not about who is the best artist, it is about the message that the artwork brings.

BASIC STEPS TO FOLLOW

Don't worry if you cannot draw or have any idea where to start. Included in this book is a template of a face that you can use as your base when drawing. You can make additional copies of this template or download the template from http://bit.ly/2QvgvpP

Meditation: http://bit.ly/2QwyFY2

- Ask your guides to step forward and give you an impression of the person to draw
- Always start with the eyes and work your way down the middle of the face to the nose, mouth, and chin
- Work then on the hairstyle and any other facial sections i.e the cheeks, facial hair and so on.
- Finish with the neck area and the shoulders and add in clothing or styles as you feel compelled.

If you see other objects, symbols and clothing add these to the side as they will have some relevance on the image

Again the goal here is for you to develop and build a rapport with your guide. The information will come into your third eye or you will just have a feeling that something needs to be drawn in a specific manner.

Go with the flow and allow yourself not to worry as to how the picture is looking but more about the connection you will be getting.

When you have developed this, then look to work with your other guides or indeed loved ones that may come through as well.

YOUR NOTES AND OBSERVATIONS

118

AKASHIC RECORDS

"Everything should be made as simple as possible, but not simpler."

Albert Einstein

i LEARNING

One of the earliest references to the Akashic Records in modern times was made by Helena Blavatsky, founder of the Theosophical movement in the late 19th century. Blavatsky claimed she learned of the records from Tibetan monks, who said the records could be found in the "akasha," or "ether," a reference to the space element in eastern five-element systems. This fifth element of space is considered the fundamental fabric of reality from which all other elements emerge — the source of material reality.

Metaphysician Rudolf Steiner also referenced the Akashic Records, asserting that every action, word, and the thought leaves a trace in etheric realms. Contemporary physicist Ervin Laszlo explores concepts of Akasha from the perspective of science, concluding that the Akasha contains templates for human ideals such as harmony and equanimity. This is reflected in his "Akasha Paradigm" which he relates to human evolutionary processes.

Those who subscribe to Akashic record models often reference the biblical "Book of Life" first mentioned in the

Old Testament (Exodus). Scripture asserts that a record of every life is kept in heaven, and it is from these records that souls are judged.

WHO CAN READ THE AKASHIC RECORDS?

This is one of those real areas that divides many people and for myself, I have to turn back to my teachings and learnings from my mentors and spirit guides.

There are those that say they can access and read your Akashic records but (again) my understanding that only those that have been permitted can read extracts of the another person's records – so what does this mean?

Firstly nobody is allowed to fully read and go through your Akashic records, past life, present or even future. Our paths are defined and as such only you can follow that path and make decisions along the way.

Secondly, you need an Akashic records guide to actually do the reading for you. The script is so ancient and not of this world, that it is impossible to decipher or understand any scripts.

I have been privileged to view my actual Akashic records scroll, and recall strange looking characters and images placed in Red and Black, but what these mean I would not be able to tell you. So understanding and meeting your Akashic records guide is something you will need to start to develop.

Thirdly only you are permitted to enter into the Akashic records to view your own records, no-one else can. This I feel causes some disruption to those that say they can access your records – I suspect that they are not and rather they are getting messages from their guides which leads me to my fourth point being our guides can access them.

It is possible for our guides to make certain information and pass on this to us as messages about a person's path or current path they are traveling. So an example would be in a Tarot reading, the messages you are given are partially coming from what has been written in the clients' Akashic records.

Of course, I would not go as so far to explain this, but there are a few rules around the messages:

- Only what the client is allowed to hear at that time is revealed

- You will only be given snippets, not a whole history

- You will only be given so much into the future and normally anywhere from 12 to 18 months is normal

YOU MUST HAVE GOOD INTENTIONS UPON ENTERING

It is possible to access your records or at least view them (although you may not understand them), through meditation. This again highlights that accessing the library is not a privilege only allowed to a handful of people, as the universe does not discriminate.

If someone attempts to enter the Hall of the Akashic Records with mere curiosity, not to mention malicious intentions, they are rejected or misinformed. The curiosity might sound innocent enough, as in "Let's find out what my boyfriend/girlfriend was like in their past lives ..." Learning who they were won't improve your relationship until you understand who you are. We always want to begin with ourselves.

And that's the biggest benefit of reading the Akashic Records: to know oneself. We like to think we know ourselves, but the fact is we don't.

Download the Akashic records guided meditation and work with this at least two to three times a month.

Use the time to work with meeting your Akashic records guide and understand the way we get to the records and the responsibility they bring.

Use the time and meditation to understand and find out more about yourself

http://bit.ly/31MvXQ5

YOUR NOTES AND OBSERVATIONS

125

PSYCHOMETRY

"I would prefer to believe that things possess the power of recall, of recollection. Those things are memoirs of the existences that once were theirs, if only we knew how to read them."

Norman Lock

Psychometry is one of many forms of scrying – or, in non-psychic terms, a way of seeing something that cannot typically be seen. Psychometry relies on touch and tangible, physical objects.

Psychometry is reading the energy of a physical object. The reading you will usually get will have to do with the object's history. It might be:

- images
- smells
- emotions
- sounds
- any of the other senses associated with memories and feeling

The object will have its own history and will also give you an idea of the history of its owner.

Most psychometrists, especially in the beginning, have to hold the object in their hands to be able to read it. Further down the line, you may be able to sense or read the object without ever having to hold it at all.

For small or lightweight objects, it is best to hold them in your hands until your skills improve. For huge or heavy objects, simply placing your hands on the item should be enough. As long as you are comfortable and relaxed, these readings should be easy and fun.

Psychometry has also been referred to as clairtangency, psychoscopy, and token-object reading, but psychometry is the most common term.

HOW DOES PSYCHOMETRY WORK?

Psychometry is reading the lingering energy and images left behind in an object. People are made entirely of energy. Our energy leaves an "energetic imprint" on everything and everyone we interact with. So, in essence, objects associated with us will hold a vibration of what has been impressed upon them – including our energy, or aura.

For a "real-life" example, have you ever written in the fog on your mirror after a shower? Your message will remain and become visible every time the mirror fogs up in the future until it undergoes a cleaning. This is similar to psychometry – the messages are not visible under normal circumstances, but with the right method, those messages remain.

When you are reading an object's energy, you are reading its aura, much like we have auras. That is what you are tapping into when using psychometry. Hopefully, the mirror analogy helped you understand a little more.

The other important thing to remember about psychometry is that objects with more meaning, and that were used more, will have more energy and therefore give better readings. It is also true that metal objects tend to hold more energy compared to other objects. Something like a wedding ring will hold more energy than a pair of gloves only worn once.

Some of the signs that you might be inclined to psychometry include:

- Antique stores make you feel weird or give off a strong vibe
- You cannot own used furniture

- You feel uncomfortable in spaces with too many objects (too much energy)
- You cannot wear old clothes or used jewelry
- Pawnshops make you feel overwhelmed
- You feel you must impulsively wash your hands after picking up used objects

If you experience any of these sensations or something similar, it might mean you would excel at psychometry. All of these are signs that you might be predisposed to reading an object's energy.

TRAINING

As with any skill, practice will always help you improve. The more you practice, the easier it will become. With the right amount of empathy, anyone can do psychometry.

Here is a basic idea of what to do when performing a psychometry reading.

1. First, wash your hands and dry them well. You do not need to be hospital sterile, but you must wash off energy that could interfere with your reading.

2. Rub your hands together to create friction and warm-up energy.

3. Now, to test if there is energy present, keep the palms of your hands facing each other and pull them apart very slowly to about ¼ inch away from each other. Is there a thick sort of sensation between your palms or some kind of energy? If so, you're all set! If not, rub your hands together some more to create more energy.

4. Pick up or hold an item in your hands. It is probably best to start with something small and personal. Any beloved jewelry works well. That will make this initial exercise much easier. It is also best if the object belongs to someone you do not have a close relationship with – for instance, perhaps ask a family friend if they have any old family jewelry you could use to practice with.

5. Relax! This is very important. You can close your eyes if you would like to.

6. Open yourself up and allow memories, images, and other feelings about the owner of the object to enter your mind. What sort of things do you sense – hear, see, smell, taste?

Here are some pertinent questions to ask during your exercise and for future psychometric readings, too.

- Who is the owner of this object?
- Can you get a sense of the owner's personality?
- What sort of memories and experiences did the owner have while wearing or using the object?
- Is the owner still alive or have they passed on?

Usually, especially in the beginning, the strongest energy that an object will give off are emotions. Love, hate, and fear are three of the most powerful emotions human beings experience. They are often the strongest sense we get during psychometry readings.

Another important thing to note about psychometry is that it is not just "items" that are worn or used that can be read with psychometry. With practice, things like photographs, homes, and graves might also be read with psychometry. One way to begin practicing this type of reading is with a photograph of a loved one who has passed on. It is a nice way to practice psychometry and also connect with the Spirit.

- **Do not be discouraged if your readings are inaccurate or muddled at first.** Like with all skills and most forms of psychic reading, you will get better with time and practice. Even renowned psychometrists aren't always correct, with an accuracy rate of 80 to 90%. They are still off 10 to 20% of the time.

- **Be sure not to judge impressions too quickly.** This is true if you are doing a reading for someone else, or even if you are simply practicing with an object of someone unknown to you. Though images or sensations may be jumbled and make no sense to you, they are probably significant to the object's owner or might mean something to their loved ones. Some impressions will be vague and some will be intricately detailed – take note of everything.

- **Even skeptical science says that psychometry is rooted in truth.** Anyone can perform psychometry and most experts believe it is a natural ability of the human mind, it is just a matter of practice and honing the skill. Any and all objects, particularly those with significant emotional or material meaning, hold the "vibrations" (or energy) of the past. When read correctly, our mind can interpret these vibrations. It's all about honing your skills.

135

YOUR NOTES AND OBSERVATIONS

136

MANIFESTATIONS

"Everyone creates realities based on their own personal beliefs. These beliefs are so powerful that they can create [expansive or entrapping] realities over and over"

Kuan Yin

ℹ LEARNING

If you look around you now, how much of what you see is the product of your own decisions, your choices, your beliefs about yourself?

Almost everything. And those things which you cannot explain – the negative stuff, the adversity, the misfortune – believe it or not, even that is the product of choices and decisions you've made at some level, at some time.

There are many different 'definitions' of the word manifest, but the simplest would be that a manifestation is 'something that is put into your physical reality through thought, feelings, and beliefs'.

This means that whatever you focus on is what you are bringing into your reality. You may focus and manifest through meditation, visualization or just via your conscious or subconscious.

This process is called manifesting!

For example, if you have been thinking about getting a new job and you focused on exactly what you wanted and when you wanted it, your thoughts and feelings would be strong surrounding this. You could then try to meditate or visualize your goal and this can help to manifest it into your reality.

If you then got your new job and it was everything you wanted, you would have successfully manifested it into your life.

HOW DOES MANIFESTATION WORK?

Like with the Law of Attraction, a manifestation is where your thoughts and your energy can create your reality. If you are constantly being negative and feeling down, then you are going to attract and manifest negative energy.

The first thing to do when manifesting is to take a look at your thoughts and feelings. Are you feeling negative? Do your thoughts surround negativity? If so, you could begin to manifest things you don't want in your reality. This is why it's important to clear your mind and have a positive mind when you are wanting to manifest.

Manifestation doesn't just work with your thoughts, there has to be a form of action on your part. This could be actually applying for the jobs that suit what you are looking for and going to the interviews.

Trying to visualize your thoughts and feelings about your job; this will then help you to feel more positive and motivated to make these changes a reality. This will then push you to take some action and, ultimately, manifest your goals into your life.

MANIFESTATION STEP 1: CHOOSE WHAT YOU WANT TO MANIFEST

When you decide on something specific to manifest, it's vital that you know exactly why you want this specific thing in your life. And when you're trying to manifest something in just 24 hours, you also have to pick something you believe you can manifest in a day.

So, for example, there's little point in saying you want to start a new business in 24 hours unless you actually believe you can attain this goal in the next day. However, you may well believe that you can successfully manifest the next step in your journey to a new business in a day, in which case you might set that as your goal (e.g. to complete a business plan, get a loan you need, or find someone to collaborate with).

When picking a thing to manifest, ask yourself the following questions:

- Do I really want this, in my heart of hearts?
- How will I benefit from having this?
- When I think about having this, does it feel right?
- How will it be good for me and for others?

Whatever want should be the greater good, and something you want in itself; most likely something that's a significant step on the journey towards a greater manifestation goal.

So, in sum: decide what you want, really connect with the intention to have it, and believe that you will receive what you ask for.

MANIFESTATION STEP 2: GET RID OF THINGS THAT STAND IN YOUR WAY

Unfortunately, almost always there will be something

standing in your way to success. This shouldn't scare you, this is just part of the whole manifestation process.

Keep an eye out for these three most common manifestation blocks:

- Negative beliefs/**mindset**

  If you are in a bad place emotionally, you need to first get yourself into the right mindset before you can successfully manifest anything. You can't be focusing on negativity and expect to attract good things into your life. So take some time to practice self-care. Try meditation and different stress-relief techniques.

- Toxic people

  When you are working on manifesting your dream you need to make sure no one is holding you back. People who don't believe in you, always criticize you and/or complain about everything are blocks that will keep you from doing your best.

- <u>Timing</u>

   Sometimes you just need to be patient. Everything you want will happen. but it will happen at the right time and for the right reasons. So if something isn't happening for you right now, it doesn't mean it never will. Keep believing and keep working on your goal.

Sit back and think about how your manifestation process is going at the moment.

MANIFESTATION STEP 3: VISUALIZE WHAT YOU WANT TO MANIFEST

You probably already know the basics of visualization and have at least tried to practice those techniques a couple of times. On your current manifestation quest, start by going somewhere that's quiet and private, and spend just a minute on visualizing the thing you want.

Pour all your energy and concentration into seeing it with your mind's eye, and let all the good feelings about the object or outcome well up inside you

This step works best if you do a multi-sensory visualization; if you can see, hear, smell, touch and (if relevant) taste the outcome you're looking to create. Make it as real as you possibly can, so it's almost like it's yours already.

Add as many details as you can, and don't try to imagine exactly how the thing or outcome becomes yours; instead, focus solely on the end result of receiving what you desire.

Don't think about how your desired object or outcome will manifest and don't try to see it coming to you through any particular person or means. Your focus should be on the end result of receiving the thing of your desire.

MANIFESTATION STEP 4: TAKE ACTION TO MANIFEST WHAT YOU WANT

You can spend the rest of your day pretty much living as you normally would; there isn't any particular action you need to take in order to make manifestation possible (your intentions are what will determine your success).

However, if you feel the urge to do something specific; whether it immediately makes sense or it's more of an intuition-based yearning. Then consider following your gut and taking that action. If it feels natural, do it!

If you find that you don't get the outcome you want within 24 hours or less, look back at the first two steps and go back through them. Sometimes, writing down what you want (and some of the answers to the specific questions posed) can give the universe the extra nudge it needs to fuel your manifestation.

There are some common reasons why you might not be manifesting quickly. In particular, consider whether you're doubting the process; do you either not believe you'll get what you ask for because you don't think you deserve it, or perhaps doubt whether it's possible to manifest using the Law of Attraction?

Any kind of negative feelings (e.g. anxiety, worry, anger, and doubt) or negative beliefs can inhibit your results.

MANIFESTATION STEP 5: RECOGNIZE AND APPRECIATE

Although this final step might not look that significant at first glance, it can actually do a lot to shape your manifestation potential in the future. Basically, the key thought here is that you need to fully appreciate what you have once you achieve your goal. It can be easy to forget that you asked for what you received, so take proactive steps to prevent this.

Go back to what you first thought and felt when you were visualizing your desired object or outcome, and connect those experiences with the new experience of having what you want. Consider the tangible proof you have that thoughts are things, and that thinking in a certain way can create concrete changes in the world around you.

The more you make this connection and emphasize it, the better you'll be at manifesting in the future (as you'll replace negative, limiting beliefs and doubts with confident, positive thoughts and feelings).

SIGNS YOUR MANIFESTATION IS CLOSE

When you are trying to manifest something into your life, there are many signs that you should be looking out for in order to know that your manifestation is close. Some will be small signs, and others might be staring you right in the face, without you knowing.

Here are some of the signs that may come to you when your manifestation is close:

- **Hearing about your desires.** This could be overhearing someone's conversation or listening to the radio, where they are talking about the very thing that you want.

- **Feeling excited.** If you start to develop a sense of excitement despite there not being a reason, this could be a sign that your manifestation is close.

- **You see <u>repeating numbers</u>.** Repeating numbers have important meanings and these are a good sign that your manifestation is close. Pay attention to the numbers you see.

- **Other people talking about your goals.** The people in your life might bring up your goals in conversation, telling you that you would be good at something (even if they are unaware that this is your goal).

These are just a few signs to show that your manifestation is close to being in your reality. Make sure to keep a note of the signs you are seeing and feel excited that your manifestations are close.

Exercise – Write Down one manifestation you want to happen in:

4 weeks time:

____

____

____

3 months time:

____

____

____

6 months time:

____

____

____

YOUR NOTES AND OBSERVATIONS

149

USING CHI

"Our body is a sacred temple. A place to connect with people. As we aren't staying any younger, we might as well keep it stronger."

Ana Claudia Antunes

WHAT IS CHI?

The Chinese word "chi" or "ch'i" can be defined as life force or energy and has parallels in other cultures: "prana" in India or "qi" in Japan. Developing your chi can be a way to heal your body – both physically and mentally – as well as a path to reaching your full potential. To fully realize your life force, you have to develop your breath and physical practice, and then approach the development of your chi on the level of energy and spirituality.

Indeed when I was training in the art of Wing Chun and Jet ken Do, we were taught how to focus our Chi to the palm of our hands for combat. This way, during a palm strike to an opponent, the "Chi" would do most of the damage to rather than causing pain and self-injury.

Although this may seem a little extreme, Chi can be used for good as well, and often I call upon my healing guide Chen who will use my Chi is healing.

Clients have experienced a sense of immediate change, heat and even the feeling of being generally well, uplifted and more optimistic after such sessions.

Other martial arts such as Tai Chi are a great way to develop your chi on a physical level and will help you to maintain a balanced healthier lifestyle.

WORKING WITH CHI

You can increase and develop your chi to overcome illness, become more vibrant and enhance mental capacity. The concept of a life force is found in most of the ancient cultures of the world. In India, it is called prana; in China, chi; in Japan, ki; for Native Americans, the Great Spirit.

Chi flows through pathways called meridians. There are twelve major meridians in the human body. Each of them is associated with a particular organ system such as the lungs, the heart, the kidneys, etc.

In a healthy specimen, the chi flows evenly, making the body vibrant and strong. If the chi is weak or "blocked", you may feel tired, achy, and even emotionally distraught.

TO ACTIVATE YOUR CHI – QUICK VERSION

If you have ever seen the Karate Kid, you may have seen this in the movie. Of course, even though this is fiction, there was a lot of truth to the process being shown.

1. Slap your hands together or rub them briskly to awaken the energy.

2. Bring your hands to a relaxed prayer position in front of your face but do not let them touch.

3. Focus all your energy into the center of your palms and begin to feel the sensation of a magnetic force.

4. Try to imagine a small ball of chi or light energy forming between your hands.

As your palms close in towards one another, you should notice a subtle feeling of resistance much like two magnets trying to push away from each other.

Separate your hands slightly and then close them again. Do it slowly. Practice this often so that you become familiar with how the energy feels. Later on, you'll notice it within your body.

DEVELOPING YOUR CHI THROUGH BREATH WORK

Get comfortable. To properly work on your breathing, it needs to be your main focus – not on how uncomfortable your legs are, or how you want to hang a picture on the wall you're staring at. Choose between a chair and a pillow on the floor – whichever would be most comfortable is the best choice.

In a chair, sit with your back straight, your feet flat on the ground, and knees shoulder-width apart.

On the floor, choose either a cross-legged position or kneeling.

Breathe deeply. Pay attention to breathing in and out. Make sure you are using your diaphragm, not just your chest. Breathing from your diaphragm (lower in your body, close to your stomach) allows you to get more air both in and out.

Cycling a lot of air through your body is essential to developing your chi.

Keep doing this exercise over the course of days and weeks until it becomes natural. Then you can begin to attempt this style of breathing wherever you might be to help get your energy flowing.

Keep your mind empty. It's difficult to keep your mind neutral and away from thinking about anything and everything. But for the 5-10 minutes that you are practicing breathing, try to just focus on that. The in and the out are like the yin and yang – opposites, yet interconnected.

Try breathing in a square. Not actually breathing in the physical shape, breathing in a square is for after you have mastered the basic breathing from the diaphragm. Put yourself into your comfortable seated position to begin. To breathe in a square:[3]

- Breathe in
- Hold your breath for 5 seconds
- Breathe out
- Hold your breath for 5 seconds

BENEFITS OF CHI EXERCISE

- Increased energy and vitality

- Better quality of life in old age

- Deeper, more restful sleep

- A peaceful mind and a positive attitude

- Balance in breathing, heart rate, and blood pressure

- A deep feeling of spirituality

YOUR NOTES AND OBSERVATIONS

WORKING WITH SPIRIT

"The first peace, which is the most important, is that which comes within the souls of people when they realize their relationship, their oneness with the universe and all its powers, and when they realize at the center of the universe dwells the Great Spirit, and that its center is really everywhere, it is within each of us."

Black Elk

For many people to be able to hear or even see spirit will not be possible and this will cause some level of concern or feel that your ability to do so is not inherent.

The truth is, it is not everyone's path to be able to do this and but there will be times, especially as you are working through this book, that you will notice subtle things happening around you.

As these changes occur you may decide that you no longer want to work or deal directly with spirit at this time and may want to close this part down, This is not an issue and again asking your guides to honor your wishes and asking them to block spirits coming through will be enough to do this.

The other way will be that you imagine an ON/OFF switch in your mind. When working with spirit this tends to be ON but my mentally thinking and visualizing it is in the OFF position will then stop spirit coming through.

You may ask why you need to do this. Other than feeling you are not ready, working with spirit is one of the most draining of experiences any person can go through.

You will feel sick, tired and be prone to illnesses a lot more. You will find your eyesight and hearing star to diminish along with your memory. So although working with spirit may sound 'fun' does come with a lot of responsibility and side effects that you need to consider.

WHISPERING NIGHTS

One of the earliest forms of spiritual connection is what I call the whispering spirits. You will tend to notice this more at night and when you are lying in bed relaxing. As you relax and go into a meditative sleep you will hear what sounds like whispering around you.

These voices if you concentrate enough, you will be able to hear words, phrases, accents and even other languages being spoken and although they are not connected to you or messages you need to understand, it is an early form of spiritual connection.

Occasionally you will hear your name or someone asking for help. If this is the case just ask them to step forward and ask what they need. If they respond great….if not then leave it as they will come back later.

SHADOW PEOPLE

Again this is also one of the early forms of working with spirit. You may see out of the corner of your eye a fleeting or darting dark shadow or even a person walking past in your peripheral vision.

After a time you will start to note height, age, and gender as your spiritual awakening occurs and although this may look negative in fact is not.

Interaction with shadow people is rare and they will let you know if they need help or looking for someone, but often or not they just see another Lightworker and want to interact and be with them

THIRD EYE

When working with clients or channeling using your third eye will help with a spiritual connection. Having your eyes closed will help and although clients are looking from words of wisdom and knowledge, often find that the messages are more about love, being sorry or asking how things are going.

- Working with your third eye keep your eyes closed and ask your guides to bring forward those who want to interact with the client or give the name of the client has asked for a specific person

- You should get an image almost like a movie in your head. I tend to get spirit coming through clouds or mists and tend to be wearing a suit for men, but it will be different for you.

- If you cannot get a message directly from spirit ask your guides to act as a middle person so they can help you

- Don't work too hard and you may see other images which will have a bearing around the person in spirit so just pass on what you are seeing.
- You might physically see the person and in this case, give as much detailed description that you can.
- Take your time.

AREAS TO BE CAREFUL ABOUT.

- If you are working within physical that is a person who feels the pains or spirit when they passed, then just take a note of what you are getting and pass it on. If you are not sure if the pain is yours, then ask your guides to take away the pain and it goes straight away then its spirit.
- There is a fine window of opportunity. Those that past tend to be strong within the first 6 weeks before a quiet period of around 6 months. After this, their connections tend to be a lot stronger.
- If a person was naturally quiet in life then they will be in spirit so don't push them or get frustrated.
- If the person was a suicide BE CAREFUL. You will need to call your doorkeeper forward and ask them for

protection throughout. The problem is you may take on the suicidal tendencies of the spirit yourself and this will be harmful and potentially fatal. There are known incidents of Mediums who for no reason have suddenly committed suicide after working with spirit.

- Watch your health – this is the biggest factor and one I cannot stress more about.

It is also worth noting the following:

1. There are some who will see and hear spirit
2. Some will see and not hear
3. Some will hear and not see
4. Some will neither hear or see

In the case of the fourth point, it is then when you need to work closely with your spirit guides and develop that connection.

The following meditation called Spiritual Wellness is a good way to relax and connect with spirit.

http://bit.ly/2XvaAlT

YOUR NOTES AND OBSERVATIONS

OUT OF BODY EXPERIENCE

"To be a true skeptic, one has to have first believed or given consideration to the possibility that they are in fact wrong"

Mark Howard

WHAT IS OUT OF BODY?

Sometimes referred to as Astral Travelling or Projection, out of the body at that moment when your etheric projection of yourself leaves your physical body. Once this is done laws of time, space and everything we take for granted, no longer exist and allow you to travel or go wherever you want to.

Some people have used this for Akashic record traveling, others to gain a sense of who they are and where they are heading, but most will do this as a way to connect and gain a deeper understanding of their guides and their spiritual journey.

Out of body can be induced (self-taught), spontaneous or involuntary such as an NDE (Near Death Experience).

Interestingly, out of the body is mentioned a few times in the Christian Bible and most notably by the apostle Paul.

He says in **2 Corinthians 12:1–4**, "I must go on boasting. Although there is nothing to be gained, I will go on to visions and revelations from the Lord. I know a man in Christ who fourteen years ago was caught up to the third heaven.

Whether it was in the body or out of the body I do not know—God knows. And I know that this man—whether in the body or apart from the body I do not know, but God knows—was caught up to paradise. He heard inexpressible things, things that man is not permitted to tell."

SILVER CORD

Our etheric projection is connected to our physical body via that of the silver cord. This cord is similar to a life belt and no matter the distance of your journey allows you to remain connected to your physical self.

The cord cannot be tangled but once the cord is severed then we enter into the spirit and our physical body dies.

You have to understand that as with an elastic band, the more you use the cord the more play and elasticity there is and like an elastic band, once the elasticity goes then there are the dangers of the cord being severed.

Regardless of how you work, you must always pay attention to your health as this will indicate the cord's health as well.

During out of body you may find that your physical body (more often or not) will stop certain actions. For example, you may find that you stop breathing for the duration of the experience. For you, this will feel like the experience has lasted a long time but in reality, no more than a minute would have passed within our realm.

Again it is worth noting that time does not exist outside of our bodies, and once our physical body needs to restart then you will automatically be pulled back into your body.

Sleep paralysis is often akin to out of body experiences and for many, the feeling will be strange and almost alien to you at first but after a while, you will find that it is, in fact, a pleasant experience.

WHY DO OUT OF THE BODY?

There are a number of reasons why you may want to do out of the body and for some people it is more spontaneous and a fact of life.

- Helps to you connect with your true self

- Perhaps you are intrigued and just want to try it out

- Will help you to strengthen your relationship with your guides

- To help with your spiritual growth

- To diminish the fear of death

Although the most common way out of the body is via spontaneity, it is possible to induce or create an out of body experience for yourself.

HOW TO INDUCE OUT OF BODY

The Following is known as the **Visualization method** and is the best way to get started.

1. Lie down on your back in a comfortable position. Find a quiet, comfortable spot where you can lie down without noise or distractions. You could lie down on a bed, your couch, a yoga mat, or even on the grass if you can find a cozy outdoor spot where you won't be disturbed. Try to clear your mind.

Let your hands rest on your chest or by your sides—whatever is comfortable for you.

2. Imagine yourself rising to float above the bed or floor. As you get comfortable, close your eyes. Try to picture your body gently floating upwards and hovering a short distance above whatever surface you're lying on.

Try to focus entirely on the image and sensation of yourself floating. If your attention wanders, gently redirect it.

3. Hold that position until you no longer feel the bed or floor. As you picture yourself floating there, try to feel it as well as visualize it. Imagine that there is only empty air beneath you. Keep focusing on these sensations until you can no longer feel whatever solid surface is under you.

You may need to maintain your "floating" visualization for some time before you can achieve this loss of sensation. If you find yourself losing focus, take a few deep breaths and try again.

4. Picture yourself moving around to explore the room. Once you feel like you're truly detached from the surface beneath you, imagine yourself slowly moving into an upright position. Visualize yourself walking or floating around the room, examining different objects and details of your surroundings. Try not to analyze what you're seeing or doing-- just let the experience unfold.

You may be tempted to turn around and look at your own body, but don't try it until you've gotten comfortable with the other stages of the process! Otherwise, you might disrupt the OBE—thinking about your physical body is likely to bring you back to it.

5. Practice this technique daily until you can comfortably do each step. This visualization-based OBE technique can take a long time to master, so don't be discouraged if you're not able to do it successfully at first. Practice each stage of the process repeats over time until you can do it easily and comfortably.

It may take a few months of practice to learn each stage of this technique. For example, you might need to focus at first on imagining yourself floating above your body, then reaching the point where you cannot feel the surface beneath you, and so on.

The key to all of this is relaxation and the want to do it. More often we feel we would like to do this but we have a fear or wanting to do it.

This is why the **Visualization method** is the best way to start. It allows you to control and be in control of what you are doing and where you are going as well.

For myself, I'm spontaneous out of body person and find that it is needed to connect with my guides when there is higher learning to be carried out.

I have felt myself floating above my body, walking around the home – even being able to walk through walls and closed doors.

I have also found that connecting with loved ones has played a big part in this too. On occasion, I have found myself between the planes with loved ones and those that I know that have passed over. This may seem strange but as you develop and grow this ability you will find that your out of the body will have a specific and different feeling from mine.

DANGERS OF OUT OF BODY

I have already mentioned the care with your silver cord but there are other dangers to be considered too. If you are sick or been drinking/using drugs this can have a negative effect on your experience. Likewise, if you have a health condition then this too must be taken into consideration before you start.

Sometimes you may get the feeling of not wanting to come back and this will also present problems, but your physical body and your guides will make sure you are brought back when needed.

WHAT TO DO AFTER THE EXPERIENCE.

After you have finished then make notes of your experience – date, time what you did and (if you can) how long the experience was.

Finally ground yourself and drink plenty of water as the energy used will need you to be fully replenished.

YOUR NOTES AND OBSERVATIONS

176

TRANCE MEDIUMSHIP

"Changing your words changes your mind. Changing your mind alters your energy and that is what changes your life."

Jodi Livon

A trance medium as the name suggests places themselves into an altered state of Consciousness, usually known as a "trance", with the objective of channeling information directly from beings of the inner realms.

Although trance mediums can and often do make contact with deceased humans, they have also been successful in making contact with inner-level Spirits, many of whom can provide valuable and accurate information on Spiritual matters.

Over the years genuine trance mediums with high-level channeling abilities have channeled a considerable amount of often very valuable information from Spirits of the inner spheres, some of whom have been very high-level Spirits indeed, often resulting in the information of great value to mankind.

On several occasions, these inner-level Beings have channeled information through the same medium for many years, and the information thus received has often been the subject of various series of books, many of which are still available today.

It is worth noting right now that not everyone will be a trance medium and this gift is not something that can easily be taught, however, it is worth understanding and learning about this so that IF you start to develop trance mediumship states, you will at least have some learning and protection.

POSITIVE AND NEGATIVE STATES

For myself, I recall the first trance experience that I recall when I was around 16 years of age. And although I do not recall much of it, my mother at the time was witness to the event (apparently she said it was an interesting conversation).

I'm also aware of even earlier experiences when I was around 5 possibly 6 years of age with my grandparents. In short trance, mediumship is something you will have already been doing or may have had some experience and not even realized you were doing this.

There are two states of trance mediumship and both come with their issues and also their ability to drain your energy levels very quickly. This is the main area that you need to be aware of and one that allows you to control what's going on.

Positive Trance is where I allow my guides, Hamish and Ursula, to come through. In the process (outlined in the training section), I'm taken to a higher place normally a location that is specific to myself and my guides, although recently I have been found to be taken underwater and told to wait.

During these sessions, Ursula and/or Hamish will conduct a session giving information about events and information attaining to those going forward. They have not brought forward the spirit and rightly so as I do not have control in these sessions and consequently unable to connect with my doorkeeper.

The only difference is my healing trance guide, Dr Benedict. During these sessions, I will have some control but not much and he will conduct a high-level healing session which has given some remarkable and almost instantaneous results.

Negative trance in comparison is as it would suggest when spirit tries to come through without my permission. This is dangerous and is normally very quick to occur.

In these incidents, the spirit will try to come through and take over my body and control my actions. Because of the energy that is used, it is possible that I could die from such incidents and so I have to be very careful about how I work – the trouble is you cannot be a trance medium and just work with positive trance.

The warning signs for myself are that I get a strange "dead" feeling in my right leg and that is followed by a nudge in the back – but it happens quickly. In a negative trance, the spirit will enter in via your back.

RESCUE MEDIUMS

One of the most important people you will require if you start working in trance is a rescue medium. This person is someone you trust above anyone else as they literally have your life in their hands.

The second you go into a negative trace or if you are in a positive and spirit (other than your guides) comes through, then your recuse medium has to be on hand to help you out.

- Firstly and most important NOBODY must say your name during the session. The spirit can take this information and use it to their advantage

- Next, if in a negative trace, the rescue medium MUST ask the spirit to leave and say in a commanding voice "Let me speak with the medium" and use the word now if required i.e. "Let me speak with the medium NOW!"

- They may need to repeat this and become stronger and firmer, almost like a parent or teacher reprimanding a child.

- Once you are out of the trance, bring your doorkeeper forward and protect yourself.

The following is for positive trance work ONLY. This means you will have already been introduced to your trance guide and this is the process for allowing them to come forward and speak through yourself.

1. Go into a meditative state and ensure all your chakras are closed.

2. Next, bring your doorkeeper forward and advise them that you are going to go into positive trance. Ask them to step aside and allow your trance guide to step forward

3. During the trance, your spirit/soul will be located in the place where your Doorkeeper was and take their place (now you see why this has so many dangers to it).

4. Ask your trance guide to step forward.

5. Opening your root and your crown chakras only, start pulling the red of the root up and the white crown down till they meet in the middle around about your heart chakra.

6. During this time you guide will take you deeper to mediation. They will advise how deep you are and take you away to a place where you are safe.

7. You will be taken down anywhere from 80% to 90% in a meditated state. Once you are there your trance

guide will then announce themselves and start giving their messages.

WHAT YOU WILL EXPECT TO HAPPEN

As you can see this takes a lot of energy and so this requires you to be fit, healthy and working at an optimum level with your guides and doorkeeper.

- You will find that your legs start to go dead or you cannot feel them. In fact, your body is being tricked into being told it has died and you are starting to go into a form of rigor mortise.

- You may find that you a re-disconnected as you are being moved from your body to the new location. This will make you fight it as it won't be natural and you will want to stop

- Your throat may start to become itchy or constrict during the process. Breathing will become harder to manage and you will be very short of breath during the transfer.

- Your guides will monitor the process and when ready they will take you out of the trance state slowly.

COMING OUT OF A TRANCE

1. Your guides will inform you that you are coming out of a trance.

2. You will start to become aware of yourself and your surroundings. Hearing tends to be the first thing that comes back to you.

3. Your guides will take you from the 80-90% meditative state to fully aware and awake. During this process, your red and white colours of the root and crown chakra will go back to their locations. Almost like a cloud of red being pulled down and a cloud of white being pulled up.

4. You then need to close your root and crown chakra

5. Start a grounded process and drink a lot of water.

6. Your legs might take about 10mins before you get feeling back into them so don't worry

YOUR NOTES AND OBSERVATIONS

186

RESOURCES

Meditations

Meeting Our Guides: http://bit.ly/2Ottrtx

Akashic Records: http://bit.ly/31MvXQ5

Spiritual Wellness Meditation: http://bit.ly/2XvaAlT

Beach Relaxation (can be used with Past Life):

http://bit.ly/2r8cv3M

Past Life Meditation: http://bit.ly/2Y1yyEc

Grounding Meditation: http://bit.ly/2TBk8Zy

Chakra Meditation: http://bit.ly/2SKppOz

Positive Affirmations Meditation: http://bit.ly/2Xf7Oj1

Psychic Art Meditation: http://bit.ly/2QwyFY2

Psychic Writing Meditation: http://bit.ly/35mm6Tz

Guide Sheets

Meditation How to guide: http://bit.ly/2tqFmyi

Psychic Art Template: http://bit.ly/2QvgvpP

Past Life Roadmap: http://bit.ly/343UUZw